Eight Keys to an Extraordinary Board–Superintendent Partnership

Doug Eadie

Rowman & Littlefield Education

Published in partnership with the
American Association of School Administrators

Rowman & Littlefield Education
Lanham • Boulder • New York • Toronto • Plymouth, UK

2003

This title was originally published by ScarecrowEducation.
First Rowman & Littlefield Education edition 2006.

Published in the United States of America
by Rowman & Littlefield Education
A Division of Rowman & Littlefield Publishers, Inc.
A wholly owned subsidary of The Rowman & Littlefield Publishing Group, Inc.
4501 Forbes Boulevard, Suite 200, Lanham, Maryland 20706
www.rowmaneducation.com

Estover Road
Plymouth PL6 7PY
United Kingdom

British Library Cataloguing in Publication Information Available

Library of Congress Cataloging-in-Publication Data

Eadie, Douglas C.
    Eight keys to an extraordinary board-superintendent partnership / Doug
Eadie.
        p. cm.
    "A ScarecrowEducation book."
    "In partnership with the American Association of School
Administrators."
    ISBN 978-1-57886-016-6
    1. School board-superintendent relationships—United
States—Handbook, manuals, etc. 2. School
superintendents—Professional relationships—United States—Handbooks,
manuals, etc. 3. School districts—United
States—Administration—Handbooks, manuals, etc. I. Title: Eight keys
to an extraordinary board-superintendent partnership. II. American
Association of School Administrators. III. Title.
LB2831.72.E22 2003
379.1'531—dc21

                                                        2003001744

♾™ The paper used in this publication meets the minimum requirements of
American National Standard for Information Sciences—Permanence of
Paper for Printed Library Materials, ANSI/NISO Z39.48-1992.
Manufactured in the United States of America.

For Kay Sue, Charles, Beth, William, and Matilda

Contents

Foreword

Our forebears wisely recognized that universal, easily accessible, high-quality public education was critical to the success of the noble U.S. experiment in self-government. Accordingly, public schools were among the earliest accomplishments of the settlers who populated the U.S. colonies. Well-led and well-managed public school systems are just as important to the health and vitality of our democratic institutions today as 300 years ago, but public education in this country is being challenged these days as never before—educationally, financially, socially, and politically. Of course, being challenged is at the heart of creative growth and significant innovation, and so U.S. public education can emerge from this period of testing even stronger: educationally more effective and organizationally more efficient and resilient.

Whether the more than 13,000 public school systems in the United States are to successfully meet today's daunting challenges will depend heavily on their capacity to generate what Paul Houston and Doug Eadie, in *The Board-Savvy Superintendent*, call "high impact" governing. Governing, as Paul and Doug explain in detail in their book, involves much more than the old-fashioned notion of merely creating a structure of policies (which, after all, are basically just rules) to guide district operations. Truly high-impact governing, according to Paul and Doug, involves making critical decisions that determine our school district's vision, strategic directions, major innovation targets, fundamental purposes and mission, operational priorities and goals, and how well it is performing educationally and financially.

Long experience has taught Paul, Doug, and me—and probably most of you reading this—that school boards cannot possibly govern at a high level on their own. Producing the kind of high-impact governing that your school districts must have to flourish in these challenging times requires that you build and maintain a close, positive, productive, and enduring board–superintendent partnership—a "district strategic leadership team," if you will. This is what Doug Eadie's *Eight Keys to an Extraordinary Board–Superintendent Partnership* is about. This book, along with *The Board-Savvy Superintendent*, provides you with a powerful "one-two punch" consisting of practical and tested guidance that you can put to immediate use in developing high-impact governing capacity in your district. *The Board-Savvy Superintendent* lays out in detail the work that is actually involved in governing, while Doug's *Eight Keys to an Extraordinary Board–Superintendent Partnership* concentrates on down-to-earth ways to build and maintain the kind of partnership that serves as a foundation for effectively governing.

I agree wholeheartedly with a critical assumption of Doug's that is at the heart of this very impressive book: that the superintendent must play *the* leading role in building and maintaining a close, positive, and enduring partnership with a school district's board and its CEO. One of the greatest strengths of *Eight Keys to an Extraordinary Board–Superintendent Partnership* is its practicality. Eschewing general theory and the platitudes that are so common in the governance literature, Doug draws on 25 years of hands-on experience in providing advice and counsel that you can put to good use right now in your district. I am also impressed by Doug's focus on the psychological and emotional dimension of the board–superintendent partnership, particularly his attention to practical techniques that you can employ to foster feelings of ego satisfaction and ownership among your board members and to make the work of governing enjoyable and inspiring as well as serious.

Eight Keys to an Extraordinary Board–Superintendent Partnership is well worth your time and close attention, and you will want to consult it frequently as you work with your school board. It serves as a perfect companion piece to *The Board-Savvy Superintendent*, and I recommend it to you without reservation.

—John R. Lawrence, president of the American
Association of School Administrators

The Partnership Imperative

HIGH STAKES

You can be sure that you've built a truly extraordinary board–superintendent working partnership in your school district when you can answer "yes" to 3 questions:

1. Is my school board, in close partnership with me as the superintendent and CEO of my district, producing truly high-impact governance that makes a real difference in the affairs of my district?
2. Am I effectively providing executive leadership to my district?
3. Are my board members feeling deep satisfaction as a consequence of carrying out their governing work?

Building a close, positive, productive, lasting board–superintendent partnership in your school district is a truly high-stakes matter. If you, as your district's superintendent and chief executive officer (CEO), don't devote significant time and energy to building the board–superintendent partnership, your district, you, as the CEO, and your board members will pay an unacceptable price. Your district will pay the highest cost in terms of inadequate governance, but your executive leadership will also suffer, as will your board members' governing experience.

THE GOVERNING CHALLENGE

Never has the need for high-impact school board leadership been greater. In these changing, frequently challenging, and occasionally threatening times, school boards must accomplish their governing work at a high level—grappling successfully with a never-ending array of thorny strategic and operational issues—if their districts are to succeed in carrying out their educational missions and in translating their districts' visions into reality. The governing work that must be done to assure school district success is daunting:

Updating the school district's vision and mission periodically in response to environmental change

Spotting strategic issues that are coming down the pike in enough time to address them effectively

Deciding which issues to tackle now and in the near future and investing in change initiatives to deal with them

Reaching agreement on operational targets

Rigorously monitoring financial and educational performance

You can easily add to this list of critical governing demands in these challenging times.

THE PARTNERSHIP IMPERATIVE

No school board can go it alone in accomplishing its highly complex and terribly demanding governing work. The indispensable foundation for high-impact governing is a board–superintendent working partnership that is close, positive, productive, and solid. This book is about building and maintaining that partnership in the interest of your school district's long-term success in meeting the educational needs of your community. Building such a working partnership is no easy task, in light of such factors as the complexity of governing work (and the concomitant difficulty of working out board and superintendent responsibilities in the governing arena), the inherent fragility of human relationships when large egos and "type-A" personalities are involved, and the inevitable stresses and strains that bedevil every board–superintendent partnership in today's world. However, no matter how daunting the challenge, board–superintendent partnership building should be a top priority in every school district.

But lower-impact governance won't be the only cost of failing to build a close, productive board–superintendent partnership in your district. As your district's CEO, you cannot hope to carry out your executive leadership responsibilities fully without the strong board backing, the professional stability, and the job security that depend on a solid partnership. Without such a partnership, your executive authority will suffer from the board frequently second-guessing your decisions, and your job itself may very well become a casualty.

Never forget that the people on public and nonprofit boards, being normal human beings, tend not to blame themselves for the dissatisfaction and frustration that they experience when doing their governing work, nor are they likely to consider seriously collectively firing themselves as a viable solution to a dysfunctional working relationship with their superintendent. CEOs of every kind of organization are the inevitable culprits — and all too often victims — and superintendents are no exception. Serious, sustained attention to partnership building, therefore, is critical to your executive effectiveness and professional well-being, in addition to serving the wider educational mission of your district.

You should also keep in mind that school board members can also be victims of the failure to build a strong board–superintendent working partnership. Granted, they won't lose their jobs (at least not until the next election) because of an ineffective working relationship with their superintendent. However, as volunteers who typically receive only minimal, if any, compensation for their governing efforts, the deep satisfaction that comes from making a real difference as "governors" is easily their most important form of nonmonetary compensation. The reduced governing effectiveness resulting from a dysfunctional partnership with their superintendent will, over time, ensure that frustration and irritation erode their satisfaction, depriving them of their just desserts for donating their precious time and energy to governance.

ESPECIALLY FOR SUPERINTENDENTS

Eight Keys to an Extraordinary Board–Superintendent Partnership is addressed directly to superintendents as the CEOs of their school districts for 2 compelling reasons. First, school boards cannot possibly develop into truly high-impact governing bodies, nor can strong board–superintendent partnerships be built and maintained, if the superintendent does not play the leading role in developing the board's leadership capacity and his or her partnership with the board. Of course, board members must be partners in this critical endeavor, but experience has taught that superintendents must be the driving force behind partnership building. Second, as I pointed out earlier, superintendents are typically the victims of underperforming, dissatisfied boards.

However, school board members, senior executives, and administrators will also find this book a useful resource in developing their leadership roles in the governance arena. School board members will find the very practical guidance in the following chapters pertinent both to strengthening their governing capacity and also to better understanding the nature of the board–superintendent partnership. And senior district executives and administrators can put the book to practical use in learning how to work successfully with their school boards and—for those so inclined—in preparing to become a district superintendent someday.

THE 8 KEYS

Eight Keys to an Extraordinary Board–Superintendent Partnership describes 8 down-to-earth, practical approaches that you can employ in building a board–superintendent partnership that both produces high-impact governance and also withstands significant stress in the long run. The 8 keys are not theoretical concepts; rather, they are approaches to partnership building that have been thoroughly tested in the real world and have been found highly effective in practice. They deal with both the technical content of governing work and the "softer" psychological and emotional side of what is, above all, a human relationship. You and your school board will realize the most powerful return on your investment in the 8 keys if they are put to work in your district as components of a multifaceted, integrated partnership-building program, rather than as individual initiatives.

Eight Keys to an Extraordinary Board–Superintendent Partnership is intended to serve as a companion work to Paul Houston's and my recent book, *The Board-Savvy Superintendent* (AASA/Scarecrow Press 2002). The latter work builds a foundation for using the 8 keys by delving into the content of governing work in greater detail than *Eight Keys*, which pays more attention to building and maintaining relationships. The 2 books are united by an overarching strategic assumption: As the superintendent, and chief executive officer of your school district, you are primarily responsible and accountable for building your school board's capacity to generate high-impact governance and for participating as an active partner in the governing process. You must also bear the lion's share of the responsibility and accountability for building and maintaining the kind of effective, enduring board–superintendent partnership that is indispensable to high-impact governing. Your school board must share accountability as an active partner but cannot feasibly be expected to play the leading role.

Acknowledgments

I am indebted to the hundreds of public and nonprofit boards and CEOs with whom I have worked over the years, including many school boards and superintendents. They have made it possible for me to thoroughly test and hone the partnership-building approaches and techniques that are described in *Eight Keys to an Extraordinary Board–Superintendent Partnership*. Several colleagues read and commented on the manuscript, and this is a better book as a result. In this regard, I want to thank Diana Baker, Carolyn Bricklemyer, Sheff Crowder, Alex Funari, Dr. J. Howard Hinesley, Dr. Paul Houston, Dr. John Lawrence, Dr. Earl Lennard, Dr. Roy Kaplan, Dr. Manuel Rodriguez, Cynthia Sampson, Dr. Judith Seltz, and Douglas Weber.

The National School Boards Association was an invaluable source of information on the work of school boards and the board–superintendent partnership. I particularly want to recognize Dr. Anne Bryant, NSBA executive director, and Dr. Joe Villani, NSBA deputy executive director, both of whom found time in their demanding schedules to discuss this manuscript with me. Without question, their comments and suggestions have made this book a more powerful resource for school boards and their superintendents.

My esteemed colleague and friend, Dr. Paul Houston, executive director of the American Association of School Administrators (AASA), was a rich source of wisdom and insight during the writing of this book, and co-authoring with Paul the earlier *Board-Savvy Superintendent* was excellent preparation to write this book. Not only did Paul strengthen my understanding of the educational enterprise, his powerful vision for

American public education in the 21st century also inspired me to greater effort. My work with Dr. John Lawrence and his colleagues serving on the AASA Executive Committee helped me to sharpen the concepts in this book. And I deeply appreciate the contribution of Doug Weber, president and CEO of the United Way of Tampa Bay, who was kind enough to host a luncheon roundtable in Tampa at which community leaders representing education and the wider nonprofit family discussed the manuscript of this book.

The people at Scarecrow Press were unfailingly supportive and encouraging during the writing of *Eight Keys to an Extraordinary Board–Superintendent Partnership*, and I want to thank particularly Dr. Thomas Koerner, Amos Guinan, and Jessica McCleary.

This book is dedicated to my 2 brothers and 3 sisters, not only to acknowledge the importance of their friendship and support over the years, but also to recognize the invaluable lessons in human interaction and partnership building that growing up with 5 siblings taught me. I am especially indebted to my sister Kay Sue Nagle and her husband, Jim, for their generous hospitality over the past 40-some years. Their providing me with a home-away-from-home on countless occasions made writing this and other books a far more pleasant task.

My children, Jennifer and William, have not only enriched my life, but their educational odysseys — 16 years for each and not yet over — have been a constant reminder of the ultimate purpose that this book is intended to serve. And, finally, I am indebted in so many ways to Barbara Carlson Krai — my wife, best friend, and savvy professional colleague. I have never doubted for a minute that our life together is a primary source of the creative energy that I bring to my writing and consulting work in public and nonprofit leadership.

Of course, I am solely accountable for any flaws you might find in this book.

Key 1

Put Partnership at the Top of Your List

The Main Message

You must, as your school district's superintendent and CEO, embrace building and maintaining an extraordinary partnership with your school board as one of your preeminent executive priorities, deserving your intensive time and attention and requiring your strong leadership and meticulous management.

Major Plot Lines

1. Dealing with formidable barriers
2. Serving as the chief partnership officer
3. Leading and managing a formal, detailed partnership program

NOT A PIECE OF CAKE!

Bedrock pessimism might not be the most effective leadership tool you can bring to the partnership-building arena, but being a cockeyed optimist will serve you no better—and might actually be lethal, professionally speaking. Even if you really put your mind to building a solid working partnership with your school board, devoting the requisite time and tenaciously attending to the finer details of partnership building, you've taken on a challenging job. If developing a board–superintendent partnership that is close, productive, and enduring were a breeze, frankly, we would encounter far fewer strained relationships and the average superintendent tenure would be significantly longer. The fact is, board–superintendent partnerships are not only extremely important to their school districts, but are also notoriously difficult to build, extremely fragile, and prone to deteriorate if not continuously and creatively supported and nurtured.

WHAT A CAST OF CHARACTERS!

Perhaps the most formidable barrier to partnership building is the fact that the people who tend to populate public and nonprofit boards, including those of school districts, can be quite difficult to work with. Like anyone who reaches the top in an organization, more often than not, school board members bring large egos to the boardroom and tend to be headstrong and impatient. They aren't about to be led by the nose, and if they get a whiff of condescension from the superintendent or 1 or more of the senior administrators, they will be tempted to go for the jugular. Not only are they by their very nature difficult to work with, they also bring diverse motivations and psychological makeups to their governing work.

The overwhelming majority of the thousands of board members whom I've encountered over the years have sincerely wanted to do a good job of leading their districts, and malevolence has been notable by its virtual nonexistence. However, the needs that school board members bring to their work can vary tremendously. For example, I've met school board members who aspire to play a leading role in raising educational performance; who above all want to grow in governing skills; who need to be publicly visible and expect to be personally involved in dealing with external stakeholders such as city and county government; who thrive emotionally on participation in ceremony such as awards banquets; who need contact in the "trenches" (observing a sea of shining faces in a preschool program, for example), and so on. Of course, it wouldn't make sense for you, as CEO of your district, to attempt to cater to every single motivation and need, but you had better learn to spot and understand them, and to address the ones closest to your board members' hearts.

OTHER BARRIERS

In developing the board–superintendent partnership, you face a powerful double whammy related to the substantive work of governing. First, many—perhaps even the majority—of existing and incoming school board members have only a vague, and sometimes quite wrongheaded, notion of what high-impact governing work is about and how to involve the board effectively in doing it. Second, even when your board members do get a firm grasp of the work, governing is a tremendously complex "business" that demands clear goals, well-designed structure and process, and well-honed skills. Since 1 of the most important keys to building a productive, enduring board–superintendent partnership is the deep satisfaction that board members feel when they are creatively and proactively involved in doing governing work that makes a difference in the affairs of your school district, the complexity of the governing "business" and board members' lack of knowledge do, indeed, make partnership building a much more difficult task.

Two other barriers stand in the way of building the kind of board–superintendent partnership that generates high-impact governance and withstands the normal stresses and strains of any complex human relationship: (a) a constituency view of board member accountability, and (b) a hallowed adversarial tradition that has bedeviled public and nonprofit governance for more than a century. Interviews with thousands of board members over the years have taught me that many do not bring to the boardroom the broad perspective that governing is, above all else, the job of fundamentally developing the school district "corporation" on behalf of all community residents—updating its vision, setting long-term strategic targets, allocating resources to ensure that the educational mission is being carried out fully, and other high-level leadership tasks.

All too often, the broad "corporate" perspective is mixed with competing narrow agendas that have to do with representing particular constituencies inside or outside the district structure. For example, a board member might see his or her primary role on the board as fighting against an increase in property tax millage on behalf of an antitax group, or being the point person for reducing class size on behalf of the teacher's union. In my experience, this kind of constituency focus can create a powerful centrifugal force that works against building a cohesive board governing team, thereby making partnership building a far more daunting challenge.

The adversarial mentality can be especially strong in public and quasi-public organizations such as state and local government, public transit, and public education. The members of many county commissions, city councils, and transit and school boards bring to their governing work the attitude that their fundamental role is to "keep their collective eye on the critters to make sure they don't steal the store." This attitude, which comes from the checks-and-balances philosophy embodied in the U.S. constitutional system, in a very real sense institutionalizes suspicion and distrust, thereby militating against building the kind of close board–superintendent partnership that is at the heart of good governance. Unfortunately, growing disillusionment with, and declining respect for, institutions generally in our society in the early years of the 21st century has exacerbated the situation, as has the tendency of many CEOs, including superintendents, to react to this adversarial climate by becoming more defensive and protective.

BECOMING THE CHIEF PARTNERSHIP OFFICER

The CEOs, including superintendents, who have successfully surmounted the barriers—building close, positive, productive, and enduring partnerships with their boards—have, in my experience, taken on the job of chief partnership officer as well as CEO in their organizations. When you wear the chief partnership officer hat, you treat the partnership with your board as both a top CEO priority, meaning that you give it intensive time and attention, and a very special and practical "program" for which you are primarily accountable as the program "director." Although your board must obviously share accountability for building and maintaining the partnership—keeping the partnership "program" on track and in good shape—realistically speaking, you must, as a full-time executive, carry the lion's share of the burden. As part-time, lay participants in governing your district, your board members cannot be expected to do more than be willing participants in the partnership "program" that you develop and manage.

The truly outstanding chief partnership officers whom I have observed over the years, whose partnership programs have resulted in a really solid board–superintendent working relationship, have invariably shared 4 key traits:

1. They embrace strong board leadership as a cherished value.
2. They see themselves as teammates of their board colleagues, working together as a cohesive team in carrying out the governing work of the school district.
3. They are emotionally mature, possessing the healthy egos that allow board members to "own" their governing work and to experience ego gratification.
4. And they take an expansive view the of the superintendent's role—of CEOship—that goes well beyond the traditional chief administrative focus of the job.

COMMITTED TO BOARD LEADERSHIP

Above all, the superintendents who are successful chief partnership officers, in my experience, passionately believe in the value of strong boards that generate truly high-impact governance that makes a real difference in their school districts. This belief is what drives them to target board-capacity building as one of their highest CEO priorities and to serve as active agents in helping their boards to become effective governing bodies. This commitment to strong board leadership is what keeps these superintendents from falling captive to defensiveness and protectiveness in working with their boards. Far from being preoccupied with controlling their boards, keeping them in check, and vigilantly guarding themselves and their administrators from board incursions onto administrative turf, these successful partnership officers passionately believe that helping their boards realize their tremendous governing potential in practice is one of their preeminent CEO responsibilities.

PLAYING ON THE SAME TEAM

If you want distance from your board, that is one of the easiest of all things to achieve in light of the barriers I described earlier in this chapter, but the superintendents who are successful chief partnership officers are anything but standoffish with their boards. Even though they understand that, generally speaking, boundaries separating governing and executive roles and a minimum of role differentiation make good sense from a management standpoint, these consummate partnership builders aren't driven by a fence-building mentality. The perspective they bring to their work with their boards is the "we" of teamwork, not the "you and I" of difference and distance.

They don't think of themselves in the traditional sense as merely the most senior administrative staff member in their district who is responsible for representing the district administration in dealings with a distinctly different entity called the school board. Rather, these successful chief partnership officers see themselves as occupying a hybrid position—part board member and part administrator and neither completely. They see themselves as serving with their board colleagues on a cohesive team that is engaged in playing the highly complex governing "game" in their school district. As teammates, they are preoccupied with practical ways to make the governing team more productive and cohesive, rather than focusing on rules and boundaries that differentiate and distance 1 team member, the superintendent, from the others.

This view of the superintendent's role vis a vis the school board might seem a bit radical to you and perhaps more than a little unrealistic, but keep in mind it is a philosophy and an attitude that has helped many superintendents to succeed as chief partnership builders without jeopardizing their authority and their executive effectiveness as CEOs. The successful practitioners of the partnership art are supreme realists, totally disinclined to tilt at windmills. It's not that they ignore the need for rules distinguishing between the board's and superintendent's roles and functions, it's that they view the division of labor as a minor, albeit necessary, step on the way to achieving the truly worthy goal: a cohesive board–superintendent team that generates high-impact governance and a partnership that lasts.

PRACTICING TRUE HUMILITY

Emotional maturity is a complex subject that we can't delve deeply into here, but you should keep in mind that succeeding at the work of chief partnership officer requires that you go out of your way to enable your school board members to experience the ego satisfaction that constitutes much of their nonmonetary compensation for devoting so much time and energy to your district's affairs. You necessarily look for ways to "lead from behind" so that your school board members receive public recognition and credit for their leadership efforts. You give lots of thought to assuring that their ego needs are met, not yours, which requires not only that you fashion strategies for providing your board members with ego satisfaction, but also that you are self-aware enough to spot when your own ego needs might interfere with your partnering activity. If you are vigilant, you needn't become the unwitting victim of your own emotions.

Nobody's perfect, of course, and everyone's ego at one time or another gets bruised and demands some tender loving care. Superintendents are no exception. But experience has taught that it is far easier to concentrate on meeting the ego needs of your partners and colleagues on your board if you possess what I call "true humility." True humility is anything but weakness; it is the kind of fundamental self-confidence that is a sign of a healthy ego that doesn't demand constant pumping up. Being truly humble means being comfortable playing second fiddle on occasion, staying in the wings out of the public eye while others receive the recognition and credit, even taking strong board criticism in public without being thrown on the defensive. Truly humble leaders are so fundamentally strong that they cultivate and celebrate strength in the people around them, since they don't need to be surrounded by others' weaknesses to feel good.

Now, the point of this petite lecture on what might seem like an abstruse subject to some is, first, to alert you to the potential danger of letting your ego needs get in the way of your very critical work as chief partnership officer and, second, to suggest that you should seriously consider the pursuit of true humility as a sensible CEO self-improvement target. If you are reading this, then you are certainly a human being, which means that you are almost certainly imperfect and, hence, always in some danger of being tripped up by your ego needs in your partnership building efforts. Suffice it to say that you just need to be aware of the always present danger of, and to be vigilant in guarding against, any propensity to seek undue ego gratification from your CEO work at the expense of your board partners. And, of course, consider professional help when your ego needs for one reason or another are so extreme that they are threatening to destroy the always precious and fragile partnership with your board.

SEEING THE CEO ROLE MORE BROADLY

To be successful as the chief partnership officer of your school district, you also need to take an expansive view of your CEO role, seeing yourself as far more than just the most senior administrator responsible for all internal operations and the primary conduit between your board and senior administrators. Your CEO role must also include taking on the following roles— becoming:

- your board's chief psychologist: paying close attention to the emotional needs, motivations, and psychological makeup of your board members in order to foster feelings of satisfaction, commitment, and ownership— the glue that cements the board–superintendent partnership;
- your board's chief designer: helping your board design governing process and structure that enable board members to participate proactively and creatively in making truly high-impact governing decisions—rather than merely serving as a passive audience for finished staff work—thereby producing the fundamental satisfaction that undergirds a successful partnership;
- your board's chief facilitator: actively helping your board participate effectively in putting its governing design into practice, ensuring that board members play visible, leading, creative roles in the governing process as the most powerful way to keep your partnership with your board healthy. As your board's facilitator, you concentrate on helping your board negotiate its way through process, which is a far different role from developing content, such as a draft policy statement, and merely sending it to the board.

Playing these roles might require that you acquire new knowledge, develop new skills, or hone skills that have become a bit rusty. The return on your investment of time and energy in mastering these added dimensions of the CEO role will be powerful in terms of carrying out your chief partnership officer role successfully.

LEADING AND MANAGING
YOUR PARTNERSHIP PROGRAM

As CEO of your school district, you are continuously bombarded with demands, pressures, crises; controlling your own calendar can seem like the impossible dream. No matter how committed you are to building and maintaining a solid working relationship with your board, you can very easily lose track of the diverse strategies and activities involved in keeping the partnership healthy; they can ooze away like a crustacean robbed of its shell. One reason that your partnership efforts can so easily slip away from your consciousness is that no one around you will be pressuring you on the partnership front; it's uniquely your "thing." At the most, your attention will be jerked back to the partnership by symptoms of dysfunction, such as your board—out of the blue, with absolutely no warning—refusing to adopt next year's budget, which you assumed was in the bag. Now your focus is back on your partnership with the board, but after significant damage has already occurred.

You can make use of a very common-sense device that has been thoroughly tested in the area of change management to keep your partnership efforts from being overwhelmed by the inexorable pressures of day-to-day management: make building and maintaining the partnership with your board a formal, comprehensive *program* of which you are the executive director. It's your own very practical tool for carrying out one of your highest-stake functions as CEO of your school district; no one else even has to know that you are managing such a program, although they will encounter one piece or another of it as you implement your program targets.

Like any other program in your district, your board partnership program will produce the results you want only if you give it the time and systematic attention it requires:

- Articulating clear program priorities (e.g., building strong feelings of board member ownership of their governing work)
- Setting measurable targets aimed at translating priorities into actual practice (e.g., to foster feelings of ownership by revamping the committee structure to turn committees into powerful vehicles for accomplishing the detailed work of governing)
- Developing implementation timetables for achieving the targets (e.g., securing the board president's commitment to exploring a more effective committee structure by June 30 at the latest)
- Regularly reviewing progress and, as appropriate, revising targets and timetables

Granted, there's nothing theoretically exciting about the idea of a partnership program that you, the CEO of your district, direct and manage. In fact, it's so pedestrian a concept that you might be tempted to dismiss it as being beneath your CEO radar screen. Be advised, however, that it really does work, and given the stakes involved in building a solid partnership with your board, you might very well want to get the program working for you and your board, sooner rather than later.

COMING ATTRACTIONS

The following chapters describe 7 other keys that will help you—once you have made a firm commitment to serving as your board's Chief Partnership Officer and have put your partnership program in place—to be successful in partnership building and maintenance. These keys are not theoretical concepts; they are very practical, thoroughly tested steps that you can take and approaches that you can apply in building and maintaining your partnership with the board. If you apply these keys within the framework of a well-planned and meticulously managed partnership program, you can assure that your partnership with your board generates the high-impact governing that your district needs in these changing, challenging times. In addition, you can develop the kind of partnership with your board that is capable of withstanding the winds of change that are buffeting our school districts these days and the stresses and strains that inevitably test any complex human relationship.

Key 2

Specialize in the Governing "Business"

The Main Message

Specializing in the governing "business"—becoming a true expert in every facet of governing—is one of the most critical keys to building a solid partnership with your board; otherwise, you cannot successfully help your board do really high-impact governing, depriving them of the deep satisfaction on which a strong, enduring partnership depends.

Major Plot Lines

1. Becoming the expert
2. Understanding the basic elements of governing work
3. Briefly reviewing what to avoid in the governing "field"
4. Taking a more powerful approach to the work of governing

YOU'VE GOT TO BE THE EXPERT

Governing is by definition the primary work of your school board, and one of your chief responsibilities as CEO of your school district is to help your board members accomplish governing work that makes a significant difference in the affairs of your district. This is the most direct path to your board members experiencing the deep satisfaction that will help cement your working relationship with the board. Board members who aren't actively engaged in doing really important governing work tend, over time, to grow bored, frustrated, irritated, and often quite angry, making them difficult partners at best. Boards are magnets for high-achieving types who expect their work, whether paid or not, to produce important results, and nothing is surer to alienate them than feeling unproductive and underused.

So you have no choice but to aggressively pursue developing your board's governing capacity, and you can't possibly hope to succeed if you aren't a real governing expert who knows the "business" inside out. Amateurs who casually dabble in the governing business don't make effective chief partnership officers, any more than weekend actors in a community theater company will launch a serious challenge to Stanley Tucci or Edie Falco. You can't reasonably expect your board members to master the work of governing without your help, primarily because they're only part-time participants in your district's affairs.

Many, if not most, of your board members probably have barely enough time to get through their reading for the monthly board meeting, much less to think about how they can capitalize on advances in the "field" of governance in order to upgrade their governing work. Governance is such a complex "business" that is developing so rapidly that considerable time and attention are required to keep up with advances, and most board members just aren't able or motivated enough to attempt keeping up.

Even if some of your board members are voracious readers of books on governance and avid consumers of board education and training programs, you can't afford to be less knowledgeable than these hyperactive board members. Indeed, you absolutely must, as superintendent and CEO of your district, be the expert and prime mover in the board development arena. This isn't just a matter of preserving CEO face, although you should probably avoid being perceived as having fallen behind and trying to catch up with your own board members in the quest for governing knowledge and expertise.

More importantly, public and nonprofit governance isn't a settled field with a small number of universally accepted principles and a solid body of governing knowledge. On the contrary, there are competing schools of thought about boards and their governing work, and there is plenty of bad counsel to be avoided like the plague, as I discuss briefly in the following section. You don't want to find yourself in the position of reacting to—and maybe even defending yourself against—a board member who has latched onto one of those "fallacious little golden rules" that, if followed, might actually reduce your board's governing effectiveness and, in the process, damage your relationship with the board.

I'm reminded of a horror story that I've seen repeated now and then in different settings, including public school systems. The plot is simple: (1) a CEO sits back passively while an aggressive board chair assumes leadership in developing the board's governing capacity, setting up an ad hoc governance committee that the chair heads; (2) the board chair reads somewhere that board standing committees should be avoided (by the way, a particularly dangerous bit of bad wisdom) and persuades her colleagues on the ad hoc committee to recommend doing away with committees; (3) the CEO, knowing that this is a wrongheaded notion, nonetheless can't debate it with the board chair; (4) the board attempts to govern without standing committees, but governing performance actually drops while board member frustration increases; (5) board members, forgetting—as they are wont to do—that they had bought the idea of a committeeless board in the first place, hold the CEO accountable for their unhappiness; (6) the board–CEO partnership is seriously damaged, and . . . need I go on?

The point is that the CEO *is* to blame for the situation, not because she came up with the idea of not using standing committees, but because she allowed the situation to develop in the first place. Becoming an unwitting victim is a cardinal sin in the world of CEOship!

You can only become a real expert in the governing business by spending lots of your prime time reading, listening, critically questioning and testing ideas in practice, and learning from experience. You can learn by subscribing to publications that deal seriously with governance questions, for example, the *Harvard Business Review* and periodicals published by BoardSource (formerly the National Center for Nonprofit Boards). You can take advantage of educational workshops offered by the American Association of School Administrators, the National School Boards Association, and their state affiliate associations. You can make a point of building a library of books that focus on public and nonprofit governance.

You can also learn about the governing business by observing your own school board in action, being on the lookout for what works well and what doesn't in terms of governing productivity, and board member feelings about their governing work (are they enthusiastic owners or an alienated audience?). Superintendents I know also expand their governing knowledge and expertise by serving on boards in their community, which among other things helps them understand governing work from a board member's perspective.

Whatever you do to become more of an expert in the governing business, caveat emptor should be your guiding principle when you're roaming around the governing terrain. Uncritical consumers of governance advice are taking their professional lives in their hands! At this point, I'd like to take you back to basics by looking at the essential elements of governing work; then I'll lead you on a brief tour of the governance "field," and I'll conclude by sharing an updated definition of governing work that you can employ in strengthening your board's leadership.

A BASIC LOOK AT THE WORK OF GOVERNING

One way of defining *governing work* is in terms of its content: essentially the various governing "products" that your board helps to shape, review, and make decisions about, such as a values and vision statement, an annual budget, or a policy statement. You can also define the governing work of your school board in terms of the processes that your board employs in dealing with the various governing products (for example, holding an annual planning retreat or budget work session). Content and process are inextricably linked in determining the quality and ultimate influence of your board's governing work, which can be measured in terms of the impact of your board's governing activities on the affairs of your school district. The greater the impact of your board's governing work, the deeper the satisfaction your board is likely to feel, and the easier your partnership-building task is likely to be.

Let's take as an example your board's adopting an updated vision statement for your school district. The impact of that statement on district affairs—and hence its importance as a governing "product"—obviously depends heavily on the answers to a number of content-related questions, such as: Is the vision statement a detailed-enough picture of the desired future to provide any practical guidance to district planning? Does the vision statement accurately and adequately represent the views of district residents, parents, students, faculty, administrators, staff members, and key stakeholders such as local government and the chamber of commerce? Is the vision stated in terms that are inspiring and energizing?

Sticking with the updated vision statement example, you can easily grasp the importance of the process-related concerns that must be addressed, which relate to how the vision statement was created and how the vision statement will be applied in leading and managing your district. For example, what role did the school board actually play in generating the vision statement, beyond merely taking the formal action of adopting it? Did board members participate in an intensive visioning session in a retreat, then have the planning committee polish the statement with superintendent and senior administrative assistance, after which the board adopted it? Or did the administrative team fashion a statement for review and revision by the board's planning committee, which took the finished statement to the board? Whatever approach you choose, experience has taught that the more creative and proactive a board's involvement in shaping a governing product such as a vision statement, the stronger board members' feelings of ownership of the product are likely to be.

In addition, if the updated vision statement has been formally incorporated into your district's annual planning process — as, for example, a tool for helping to identify and select strategic issues demanding high-level attention — then the vision is much likelier to influence district affairs than if it is merely included in a little-consulted planning tome collecting dust on the shelf. Before examining in greater detail a contemporary approach to governing that weaves together these basic content and process concerns in generating truly high-impact governance, I want to take you on a brief tour of the traditional governing terrain, focusing on a narrow view of governing as policy making that you will want to avoid in working with your school board.

AVOIDING TRADITIONAL TRAPS

In *The Board-Savvy Superintendent*, Paul Houston and I noted that, although public and nonprofit boards have been around for a century or more and, in theory, are seen as the pinnacle of their organizational hierarchies, in practice, boards have not been the subject of truly serious attention, at least not until fairly recently. I suspect that this is partly due to board members' being part-time volunteers—by definition "lay" people—whose work pales by comparison with the "professional" (and well-remunerated) work of executive management and administration. If you doubt that the governing business has been the victim of inattention, check it out by going into any major bookstore and asking to see the books on boards of any kind—for-profit, public, nonprofit. You'll be fortunate to locate 4 or 5 after a bit of a search, while you'll find shelves filled with volumes addressing every last aspect of executive leadership and management.

The governing literature has for most of this century been scant and filled with dubious wisdom and what Paul and I call "fallacious little golden rules" that you follow at your peril. Very often these "rules" reflect a kind of damage-control philosophy that many traditional administrators hold dear. It goes like this: "My board is a different animal from me and my administrative staff, and a dangerous beastie at that, capable of wrecking havoc if not kept corralled. If I don't make sure there are clear boundaries separating me and my team from the board beastie, and guard those boundaries vigilantly, keeping my board under control and corralled in its own territory, its ugly tentacles will reach out, grab administrative work, and consequently really muck things up."

Any number of "fallacious little golden rules" have been based on this inherently negative, adversarial, anti-partnership philosophy. One is that small boards are preferable to larger ones, which is true if your preeminent concern is efficiency (it's easier to get them together, and they require less administrative support if there are fewer of them), but which isn't at all true if you're talking about strategic decision making, which thrives on diversity, and ties to the wider community. Another is that staff work going to a board should be "finished," which is certainly true if you define governing as thumbing through somebody else's work, but not a virtue at all if you want to capitalize on the experience, intelligence, and diverse perspectives of your board members or to build their feelings of ownership. This sad litany could go on and on. Suffice it to say that you shouldn't uncritically accept advice in the field of governance!

Despite the best efforts of the American Association of School Administrators and the National School Boards Association, we have a long way to go before achieving wide understanding of, and commitment to, a common "governing body of knowledge" that supports truly high-impact governing that makes a significant difference. The persistence of a traditional, patently wrongheaded view of governance proves the point. This outdated view sees governing narrowly as essentially a matter of "policy making." As any "board-savvy" superintendent well knows, no school district needs more than a handful of policies—which are by definition broad rules to govern district operations—that merit serious board attention.

An example is a policy spelling out graduation requirements. Once the few broad policies such as this have been made, they need to be updated only periodically (and usually very infrequently). If policy making were, indeed, synonymous with governing, board members would have very little to do, raising the specter of idle hands (of type A people no less!) casting about for something to fill the vacuum, and, God forbid, coming up with administrative work to do.

UPDATING OUR VIEW OF GOVERNANCE

In *Extraordinary Board Leadership: The Seven Keys to High-Impact Governance* (2001), I offer a definition of board governing work that captures far more of the potential richness of governing as a leadership tool than the old-fashioned notion of governing as policy making. This broader, more nuanced definition also presents you and your board with more opportunities to build board member feelings of satisfaction and ownership, thereby facilitating the partnership-building process. When a school board does governing work according to this definition, it plays the leading role—in close partnership with the superintendent and senior administrators—in answering, on a continuing basis, 3 fundamental questions about our school district:

1. Where do we want our school district to head, and what do we want it to become—over the long run?
2. What do we want our school district to be now and in the short run?
3. How well is our school district performing: educationally, administratively, and financially?

In the next chapter, I provide detailed guidance aimed at empowering your school board by expanding its capacity to do governing work along the lines of this definition. For now, I just want to elaborate a bit on the definition to make sure you have it firmly within your grasp. Note, first, that your board isn't seen as—alone—answering the critical 3 questions; rather, it plays the "leading role—in close partnership with the superintendent and senior administrators." By this definition, governing is a shared responsibility, but the board is seen as playing the leading role, rather than merely serving as a passive audience for finished staff work.

Note also that this definition leaves us a fair amount of work to do in what we might call "operationalizing" the governing work, which involves answering 2 critical second-stage questions:

1. What decisions does your board make relative to what particular governing "products" (e.g., the decision to adopt the annual budget)?
2. What processes does your board employ in making these decisions (including playing a role in shaping, as well as reviewing, particular products)?

Defining in detail the governing "products" deserving your board's attention and mapping out the steps involved in shaping and making decisions about these products puts in place a large part of what we might call your board's "governing design," which is the subject of the next chapter.

Key 3

Empower Your Board

The Main Message

Empowered boards make the strongest, most reliable allies for superintendents. The preeminent way you can empower your school board is to take advantage of every opportunity to involve it creatively and proactively in doing truly high-impact governing that makes a real difference in the affairs of your district. You can also empower your board by developing the people serving on it. By contrast, merely paying rhetorical homage to the concept of an empowered board—without having built a foundation consisting of well-designed governing work and board members who are prepared to govern—is a surefire path to a broken board–superintendent partnership.

Major Plot Lines

1. Making a serious commitment to empowerment
2. Involving your board in updating its "governing design" in the interest of higher-impact governing
3. Taking advantage of opportunities to involve your board creatively and proactively in doing high-impact governing work
4. Developing the people on your board

SERIOUS EMPOWERMENT

The term *empowerment* is freely tossed around these days, and the idea of being "empowered" is quite appealing for obvious reasons. (Who wants to feel "powerless"?) Unfortunately, empowerment has so often been employed as a political slogan in recent years that the term has taken on a rather sinister cast (many readers are likely to blanch at the thought of an empowered school board). And the term can feel even more threatening because of the absence of any commonly accepted definition of what "empowerment" means. However, you have every reason to devote significant time and energy to empowering your school board as one of your most important partnership-building strategies. You can empower your board by helping it become a governing body that:

- does governing work that is truly high-impact in the sense that the board's decisions really do make a significant difference in the affairs of your school district;
- plays a proactive, creative role in making governing decisions, rather than merely serving as an audience for finished staff work;
- consists of people who are knowledgeable and skilled in the governing "business."

The reason you really don't have any choice but to pursue board empowerment as a relationship-building strategy is simple. Board members who are empowered along the lines described above tend to take deep satisfaction in their governing work, and board members who feel less than powerful in carrying out their governing role are likely eventually to grow frustrated and even angry, making them prime candidates for adversaries rather than partners. This makes good sense when you reflect on the kind of people who are elected or appointed to school boards. They might not always be likeable, but they are more often than not ambitious, strong willed, and accustomed to making a difference. Over the years, I've interviewed thousands of board members, many of whom have lamented over the wide gap between their experience as board members and their much more satisfying life outside the board. Over and over, I've listened sympathetically as board members have confided that "I'm not sure what I'm supposed to be doing on the board," "I can't figure out what difference I'm making," and "I make important decisions every day in my job but feel like I'm being led around by the nose by the superintendent and her executive team."

I've never come across a superintendent or any other CEO who has consciously wanted to foster feelings of powerlessness among his or her board members. The problem lies in inattention to empowerment as a top priority and the failure to employ well-thought-out strategies for board empowerment, not in the ill intent of the superintendent. Take, for example, the notorious example of annual budget preparation. Of course, all boards, including those of school districts, must formally adopt the annual budget for the coming year. However, merely sending to the board—as I've seen many CEOs, including superintendents, do over the years—a finished budget document, laying out line-item expenditures by programs and organizational units, does not automatically empower a board, even if the budget has gone through a finance or budget committee before coming to the board.

Now, a budget document is patently an administrative tool for managing your school district, and in-depth board involvement in creating the columns and rows of numbers would clearly be inappropriate, blurring the distinction between governing and managing. However, a superintendent who really cares about board empowerment will look for practical "governing levers" that board members can pull in shaping the budget document before its submission to the board as a finished document. For example, one superintendent I know has built a prebudget board work session into the budget preparation process, which engages board members in creative dialogue with department heads on major operational planning issues, including anticipated major expenditure increases, on which school board input is encouraged. Such input is then taken into account in producing the full-fledged budget document.

If you are seriously committed to board empowerment, you can pursue 3 broad strategies to empower your board:

1. Involve your board actively in updating a "governing design" that promotes truly high-impact governing.
2. Assist your board in playing a creative, proactive role in carrying out its high-impact governing design.
3. Help your board develop itself as a human resource.

INVOLVING YOUR BOARD IN ITS OWN DESIGN

In my discussion of Key 2 in the previous chapter, I defined the work of governing in general terms as playing the leading role in answering—on a continuous basis and in close partnership with the superintendent and executive staff—3 critical questions: Where should our school district be heading in the long run? What do we want our school district to be now and in the short run? And how well is our school district performing? Helping your board flesh out what I call its governing "design" in the interest of higher-impact governance is the first major step that you can take in order to translate this broad definition into actual practice, and it is the preeminent path to empowering your board. Your board's governing design consists of its role, its detailed governing work, and the structure it employs in carrying out this work.

A well-tested approach to updating your board's governing design—its governing role, work, and structure—is to involve the board, along with the superintendent and senior administrators of your district, in a daylong work session (or retreat), at which the key elements of the governing design are worked out in rough form, after which a board committee can refine the design for formal board adoption. Of course, you could merely send a report to your board recommending that it take certain steps to strengthen its governing design, or attempt to "teach" an improved design in a board workshop, but such approaches have proved notoriously ineffective because they fail to generate the feelings of ownership on which strong board commitment depend.

At a governing design work session:

- participants can familiarize themselves with contemporary advances in the field of public/nonprofit governance;
- the key elements of a board "governing mission" can be identified;
- the work of governing can be fleshed out in terms of the ongoing governing decisions and "products" that the board should pay attention to and of the processes that should be employed in dealing with these decisions and products;
- needed enhancements in board structure can be identified.

Of course, getting your board to agree to spend a day together considering practical ways to strengthen its governing design can be a challenge. Some board members are likely to believe that the board is already performing quite adequately the way it is, some might be heavily invested emotionally in current structure and practices ("What do you mean this isn't the right committee? I've chaired it for the past 3 years, it works well in my opinion, and I'm not about to have you monkey around with it!"), and most, if not all, board members will resent committing the time. However, without spending the day together, it will be very difficult to build the understanding and commitment necessary for moving to a more effective governing design.

If you can turn a number of board members into governing design "champions" who are willing to go to bat for the governing design session, the odds of its actually being held will go way up. Most important in this regard is your board president (chair), whom you might convince to make updating the governing design of the board one of the top priorities of his or her "regime," preferably its hallmark. And you have a fallback position that I have seen work well. The board president might appoint a "governance design task force," consisting of selected board members to do the detailed design work, which can then be presented and discussed at a 2- or 3-hour special board work session. Even this more modest approach is infinitely preferable to merely attempting to sell a set of recommendations to your board that they haven't played a serious part in developing.

UPDATING YOUR BOARD'S GOVERNING MISSION

Boards are by definition organizations—people working together through formal structure and process to achieve a common mission. In this regard, one of the first and most important steps that can be taken to update their governing design on the way to greater organizational effectiveness is to develop and adopt a board "governing mission." The key elements of the mission might be brainstormed at the governance design retreat, refined and fleshed out subsequently by a board committee, and formally adopted by resolution at a board meeting. You can think of your board's governing mission as a high-level job description consisting of the board's major governing responsibilities. Your board's governing mission sets the board's sights as a governing body, indicating where board time and attention should be directed and providing a framework within which the detailed governing work of the board can be developed. Once formally adopted, the mission can also be used as an important orientation tool for new board members, who will very likely have only the vaguest idea of what governing is all about.

The idea of the governing mission isn't to establish hard and fast functional boundaries separating "pure" board work from so-called executive or administrative work. No board can carry out its governing functions effectively without the active collaboration and support of the superintendent and executive team, and the work of governing in the real world—as opposed to theory—is shared between the board and its executive staff. Rather, your school board's governing mission is intended to indicate where the board should direct its time and attention. You can state the governing mission in terms of functions (for example, "reach agreement with the superintendent on his or her annual leadership priorities") or in terms of outcomes of board governing activity (for example, "a detailed, agreed-upon set of superintendent annual leadership priorities"). Employing the outcomes mode, the governing mission might consist of such elements as:

- compliance with state laws and regulations applicable to our district;
- clear, detailed educational priorities;
- widespread public understanding of and support for our educational mission;
- regularly updated strategic development targets;
- a detailed plan for generating adequate financial support for our district.

DEVELOPING GOVERNING WORK

In my discussion of Key 2 in the last chapter, I suggested that mapping out the detailed governing work of a school board essentially involves—within the framework of our definition of *governing* (see above) and an updated governing mission—first, identifying the specific governing "products" about which the board makes decisions when it governs and, second, determining how the board will go about shaping and making decisions about these products. In this regard, the decisions and products tend to fall into 2 broad governing streams:

1. Planning
2. Performance oversight

Board empowerment is essentially about helping your board to identify the highest-impact governing products that it should be paying attention to and ensuring that it plays as creative and proactive a role in shaping these products as it feasibly can, taking full advantage of the board as a resource. In the area of planning, for example, it goes without saying that long-term strategic development targets for your school district are among the highest-impact governing products that your board could be involved in shaping and making decisions about. A superintendent little concerned with board empowerment might be tempted merely to draft a set of strategic targets and send them to the board for its review and approval. In today's world, of course, such a superintendent isn't likely to last long on the job since the board will soon become deeply dissatisfied with its governing work and, quite appropriately, hold the superintendent accountable for its dissatisfaction and frustration.

A more board-savvy superintendent with a strong commitment to board empowerment will know enough to work out with the board a process that involves the board more actively in shaping the targets. For example, your district's annual planning process might commence with a 1½ day strategic planning retreat at which major issues in your district's external and internal environments are assessed and, in the context of this updated assessment, potential new strategic development targets are identified (for example, significantly raising the graduation rate or building a closer working relationship with the county government). The kind of creative and proactive involvement that empowers your board might include: the board's brainstorming potential targets at the annual retreat; the board's planning committee refining the targets with executive staff participation and support after the retreat; and the board's eventually adopting the updated strategic targets recommended by the planning committee after thorough discussion at a special board work session.

BOARD STANDING COMMITTEES

Structure is a key element of your school board's governing design. Some aspects of school board structure are typically inflexible, such as the size of the board, the frequency of board meetings, and the method of electing or selecting board members. However, the use of standing committees is usually, if not always, a matter of board discretion, and experience has taught that well-designed standing committees can make a powerful contribution to high-impact governing. Experience has also taught that a poorly designed committee structure can be a major impediment to your board's doing high-impact governing and is probably worse than having no standing committees at all.

Well-designed standing committees enable board members to divide the detailed work of governing and to gain in-depth expertise in doing governing work, as well as provide a venue for intensive board-staff interaction that is not feasible at regular board meetings. I will take a closer look at committees as a vehicle for building board member ownership of their governing work in the next chapter as part of my discussion of Key 4. For now, I will just point out some key characteristics of well-designed committee structures that really do facilitate strong governance:

- Committees correspond to broad governing functions (for example, planning and performance oversight) rather than narrow administrative functions (such as personnel or finance) or programmatic areas (such as instruction and athletics). Keep in mind that narrowly constituted "silo" committees not only chop your board's work into chunks related more to administering than governing, they also tend to turn your board into a kind of super technical advisory committee, inviting it to meddle in programmatic and administrative matters.
- An executive or "governance" committee headed by the board president and consisting of the other standing committee chairs takes primary responsibility for ensuring that the board functions as an effective governing body. For example, this committee can help to promote the election or appointment of qualified persons to fill board vacancies, might coordinate the work of the other standing committees, and might monitor the performance of board members and of the board collectively.
- All board members serve on one and only one standing committee, with the exception of the standing committee chairs, who also serve on the executive or governance committee. This is one of the most important ways to ensure in-depth attention to governance matters and to avoid stretching board members too thinly.
- The superintendent assigns a member of the executive team to serve as the chief support person for, and liaison with, each of the standing committees.

• The only path to the full board agenda is through the standing committees, which arc responsible for introducing all items and making all reports at regular board meetings.

DEVELOPING THE PEOPLE ON YOUR BOARD

Since the people on your school board, rather than some kind of governing machine, actually shape governing products and make governing decisions, you can further empower your board by developing it as a human resource:

• Assigning board human resource development to a standing committee
• Helping to ensure that the right people fill board vacancies
• Strengthening the governing knowledge and expertise of board members
• Melding board members into a more cohesive governing team

Unless one of your board's standing committees takes accountability for developing the people on your board, board human resource development is unlikely to bc handled well, if at all. Many boards around the country have assigned this function to the executive (or governance) committee in light of its responsibility for the overall functioning of the board. One fairly simple step that the executive committee can take is to develop a profile of the ideal school board in terms of composition (the mix of members—for example, corporate executives, parents with kids in the schools, representatives of community groups, etc.) and of the attributes and qualifications of individual board members (for example, being team players, having access to key community groups). Although school boards are either appointed or elected, rather than being self-appointing like many nonprofit boards, nothing prevents your school board from adopting such a profile on the recommendation of its executive committee and making it available widely in the community or sending it to appointing authorities. At the very least, it can stimulate thinking about the human resource dimension of governing your school district.

Board members' governing knowledgc can be strengthened and their governing skills sharpened by various means under the leadership of the executive committee. For example, a library of books and periodicals dealing with governance matters can be created and items can regularly be circulated among board members. In addition, the annual strategic planning retreat that kicks off the annual planning process of your district might always have a governance education component, and board members might be encouraged to take advantage of educational opportunities offered by such organizations as the National School Boards Association and the American Association of School Administrators.

The most productive means of melding your school board's members into a more cohesive governing team is to engage them actively in doing high-impact governing work. This is the foundation stone of an effective board team, without which other team-building efforts will go for naught. Building on that foundation, however, your board might strengthen itself as a governing team through such means as developing and adopting a simple set of team interaction rules, which the executive committee can monitor (for example, publicly supporting any action taken by majority vote of the board whether you agree with it or not), or even occasionally having a professional facilitator take board members through formal team-building exercises. Just never forget that, no matter how inspiring your board members might find their Outward Bound-type experience to be, the glow will soon wear off if they aren't regularly engaged in doing high-impact governing work when they return to the district.

Key 4

Turn Board Members into Owners

The Main Message

Ownership is one of the most powerful forces for good in human affairs, including board–superintendent relations. Even if your board's governing design—its role, work, and structure—has been meticulously updated, if board members don't feel like real owners of their governing work, their commitment to governing—and to their partnership with the superintendent—will be tenuous. Strong feelings of ownership in the governance realm come from meaningful involvement in generating—not just reacting to—governing products.

Major Plot Lines

1. Making ownership a top superintendent priority
2. Coming up with creative design solutions
3. Employing board standing committees as ownership engines
4. Treating your board president as a primo owner

TAKING OWNERSHIP TO HEART

Let's say that you and your school board have reached agreement on tackling a really high-stakes strategic issue: district expenditures projected to exceed revenues within 3 years, after which forecasts show the gap

widening quickly if aggressive action isn't taken in the very near future.
The board agrees with you that a sophisticated, comprehensive strategy
needs to be fashioned. You and your board concur that, rather than just
jumping on the property tax increase bandwagon, the district must not
only consider a variety of revenue enhancement and cost-saving strategies, but also treat this seemingly negative situation as an opportunity to
strengthen the district's image and to foster strong partnership with key
community stakeholders.

As superintendent of the district, you face the challenge of designing a
process and structure that will, in a full and timely fashion, generate effective strategies that can be implemented soon enough to avert the disas-
ter looming on the horizon, while also laying the foundation for long-term
financial stability. Actually, you must grapple with two design challenges:

- first, you must deal with the technical challenge of designing a planning
  process capable of generating and rigorously evaluating a variety of
  strategies aimed at revenue enhancement and cost reduction;
- second, you must ensure that the need to build strong owners—not only
  your school board, but also key community groups whose support will
  be critical—is factored into the planning process design.

As a board-savvy CEO, you know that if you merely hire a consultant
or use staff to put together a comprehensive fiscal stability plan and send
it to your board for review, you'll turn the board into an audience that, at
best, will sit back and pick the plan apart and, at worst, will rise to the
challenge of rewriting it on the spot, or perhaps even send you back to the
drawing board to start all over. And once you've got an approved plan in
hand, it's highly unlikely that your board's commitment to carrying it out
fully will be strong enough to get you through some really tough decisions
that must be made in implementing the plan (such as actually making all
of the planned cost reductions or getting the property tax increase on the
ballot). You know that you can't afford to keep your board and other key
stakeholders at a distance, treating them as an audience, because only if
they feel like real owners will they make the kind of commitment that will
endure through the inevitable vicissitudes down the road.

I've chosen a dramatic example, but what you need to keep in mind is
that your board's being a steadfast partner and creative collaborator in lead-

ing your school district depends heavily on your board members feeling like owners, not just when you're grappling with a strategic issue involving huge stakes, such as in the example above, but also day after day after day. By turning your board members into owners on a variety of fronts, including fairly routine governing work, you will build a line of credit that can be drawn on in higher-stakes situations. In practical terms, this means that you must keep your eyes open for opportunities to build feelings of ownership all the time, viewing every process that your board is engaged in—from developing the annual operational plan and budget for the next year to merely presenting the financial report at next week's board meeting—as an opportunity to turn your board members into stronger owners. Of course, if you want strong commitment and support for a course of action from anyone, not just your board but also other critical stakeholders— your executive team, administrators, faculty, staff, and key community groups—you must turn them into owners of the course of action. I use the term *stakeholder,* by the way, to mean any person, group, or organizational entity with which it makes sense for you or your district generally to maintain a relationship because something important is at stake (such as financial and political support). The point is, you always have a design choice whenever you collaborate with stakeholders in going through any kind of process (strategic planning, budgeting, image building). You can ensure that the process fosters feelings of ownership among the stakeholders involved or you can allow the more distant audience mentality to develop.

DESIGNING OWNERSHIP INTO PROCESS

So, wearing your process designer hat, you capitalize on every opportunity you can identify to strengthen feelings of ownership among your board members—collectively and individually—as this is one of your most powerful strategies for building the kind of strong partnership with your board that will endure the test of time. In doing so, you must keep in mind the preeminent ownership design principle: If you want someone or some entity like a board to feel like the owner of a course of action, a product, a decision—of anything—you must get them involved in generating or shaping that course, product, or decision, rather than merely reacting to your best thinking. Owners and audiences are mutually exclusive!

As a designer of process, you should also keep in mind the fact that you don't want your board—or any other important stakeholder—to feel ownership of everything you or your school district are engaged in. You want to pay closest attention to processes involving high stakes and requiring strong board support, such as the fiscal planning issue described above. You wouldn't want, for example, to attempt to build board ownership of the detailed numbers in the budget document. Instead, you should focus on the board's becoming an owner of the operational priorities and performance targets that drive the budget.

Indeed, considerable harm has been done by superintendents and other CEOs who have unwittingly fallen into the trap of describing the detailed line-item financial budget document itself as the board's "primary policy expression." What this does, in my experience, is invite board ownership of the columns and rows of numbers—and the detailed objects of expenditure, meaning that board members will want to dive into the detail. Choose your candidates for board ownership carefully or risk getting your board involved in what are truly administrative matters.

Let's return to the example of the school board and superintendent who have agreed that the district must come up with a comprehensive strategy for building the district's long-term financial stability, in light of the impending large gap between projected expenditures and revenues. The design challenge for the superintendent, as CEO, is to put a planning and implementation process and structure in place that will not only generate technically viable strategies, but also foster the degree of ownership among board members and other stakeholders on which implementation heavily depends. In a very similar situation a few years ago, a superintendent with whom I was working designed the following ownership-building features into the planning process:

- The board's planning and development committee was unambiguously designated the "steering committee" for the planning effort, responsible for clearly defining the desired planning outcomes, adopting the planning methodology and calendar, monitoring progress, reviewing interim planning reports and providing guidance, and reviewing and recommending the finished recommendations to the full school board.

- The planning and development committee held a kickoff work session with the superintendent and the district's top executives, at which the desired outcomes of the planning effort were identified and the planning methodology and schedule were worked out. It was decided, by the way, to establish 4 task forces consisting of community volunteers to assist in identifying and analyzing possible initiatives aimed at building long-term district financial stability, and the committee adopted the formal charge to the task forces.
- The planning and development committee met several times during the planning process to review preliminary initiatives and provide further guidance, and the 3 special full board work sessions were held for the purpose of bringing the board up-to-date on planning progress and securing board feedback on preliminary strategies.

By the time the full-blown report from the planning and development committee was submitted to the board for review, board members were anything but caught off guard. On the contrary, regular updates and opportunities to provide feedback ensured that board members were much more than a receptive audience for the report; they were knowledgeable and supportive owners of the finished financial strategies and strongly committed to their implementation.

A THOUSAND SMALLER WAYS

That you need to figure out how to involve your board in dealing with high-stakes strategic issues, such as the long-term fiscal strategy discussed previously, in ways that will strengthen board members' ownership of both the process and the outcomes it will generate is a bit of a no-brainer. Keep in mind, however, that day after day in myriad smaller ways you can take advantage of opportunities to strengthen your board members' ownership of their governing work, primarily by involving them in district affairs in ways that provide them with the ego satisfaction that is at the heart of ownership. To do this well requires that you always keep the objective of strengthening board ownership high on your list of major to-dos and that you are continuously on the lookout for opportunities to provide your board members with ego-satisfying involvement.

Over the years I've seen highly successful CEOs, including many superintendents, foster feelings of ownership among their board members by employing such simple, low-cost techniques as:

- featuring board members prominently at major ceremonial occasions in your district, such as the ribbon cutting at a new elementary building or the annual faculty convocation kicking off the new academic year;
- giving your board members positive media exposure—everything from making sure that newspaper articles on notable district achievements quote board members and give them credit for accomplishments to "booking" board members to appear on radio and TV community affairs programs;
- employing your board members as speakers at meetings of such civic organizations as the chamber of commerce, Rotary, and women's city club;
- inviting board members to attend relationship-building meetings, and even negotiation sessions when appropriate, with such key stakeholders as the mayor and county council chair.

One caveat, which I'll discuss in greater depth in the next chapter: Whenever you ask a board member to speak on behalf of your district in a public setting, such as the monthly Lions Club luncheon meeting or on a morning radio talk show, you've got to do everything you can to ensure success. Appearing uninformed or inept, or even uncomfortable, in public is the path to embarrassment or even humiliation—feelings that are guaranteed to drive out ownership in an instant. So it behooves you to brief your board members thoroughly before any appearance, to provide visual aids when appropriate (such as an attractive PowerPoint presentation), and even to stage rehearsals when the stakes are high enough (and they almost always are).

Over the years I've learned that many highly successful and self-confident people have no idea how to use a slide presentation effectively and desperately need coaching (even if you describe it as "fine-tuning"). This point was brought home to me again recently when I attended the rehearsal of a task force consisting of 6 board members who were to present their recommendations to the full board at their regular meeting the next morning. A very attractive PowerPoint presentation had been put together, and all 6 task force members had had plenty of time to familiarize themselves with the points on the slides. As might have been predicted, 2 of the 6 task force members had prepared detailed notes, which they (until gently but firmly admonished) intended to read as they advanced the slides, looking down at the notes rather than at the audience. Another task force member believed that anyone could read the slides, and so he could just skim over the points without making them explicitly.

At the end of our 2-hour dry run, we collectively thanked our lucky stars that we'd taken the trouble to rehearse. As the CEO told me afterward in the parking lot, "Oh, you should have heard the whining about having to spend the time tonight, but they'd never forgive me for tomorrow's lackluster performance if we hadn't taken the trouble to practice."

MAKING USE OF BOARD STANDING COMMITTEES

Not long before writing this chapter, I sat in on a meeting involving a board's performance oversight committee, the superintendent, treasurer/chief financial officer, and comptroller. The major agenda item under discussion was the quarterly financial report, and the participants, over the course of a couple of hours, demonstrated why well-designed standing committees can serve as very effective vehicles for turning your board members into active owners. The first task at that meeting was for committee members to understand the report inside out, identifying actual and potential trouble spots and discussing with the superintendent and his staff what steps would be taken to address them. This very active and probing discussion, which could not possibly have taken place at a full board meeting, without question prepared the committee chair to take the lead in presenting the report and addressing questions at the upcoming board meeting.

But I saw something even more impressive happen over the course of the 2-hour committee meeting after the discussion of quarterly financial performance ended. One of the committee members asked why the report was so difficult to read, observing that "you almost need to have an accounting degree to make sense of the rows and columns of numbers, and

I feel like I should bring a calculator to meetings." "Wouldn't it make sense," another member asked, "to prepare a summary report using easy-to-read bar charts comparing actual to planned expenditures by major activity and program areas?" A fascinating discussion of the capacity of the accounting software that the district was using to produce the kind of reports that committee members wanted led to a decision to establish a staff task force to come up with recommendations for making the quarterly reports more "board-friendly." The committee agreed to hold a special half-day work session 2½ months from then to review the preliminary task force report.

This impressive meeting reminded me that well-designed standing committees can not only help to empower your school board, as I discussed in the last chapter, but can also serve as effective vehicles for turning your board members into strong owners of their governing work. For one thing, committees offer a venue for getting into the detailed work of governing in enough depth to build the real understanding on which ownership depends. As the foregoing vignette also demonstrates, committees enable board members not only to dig into their governing work, but also to influence how they carry it out. The performance oversight committee both prepared for the upcoming board meeting by reviewing the quarterly financial results in detail and set into motion an effort to strengthen the monitoring process itself, further strengthening board members' ownership of their monitoring function.

Standing committees also foster feelings of ownership by showcasing their chairs at full board meetings. You can assure this by requiring that committee chairs and occasionally other committee members make all reports and introduce all action items at full board meetings, with no exceptions. Not only does this rule foster ownership by providing committee members with ego satisfaction, it also requires committee members to prepare for full board presentations, further strengthening their ownership of their governing work. Of course, if your board decides to showcase committee chairs and members in this fashion, you must make sure that they are well-prepared to play this role effectively at full board meetings. The failure of a committee chair to perform well in public will cause embarrassment, which is sure to breed resentment rather than ownership.

FIRST AMONG EQUALS

Board-savvy superintendents recognize that their district president, as chair of the school board, is not only one of their highest priority stakeholders, but also their preeminent partner in both board development and district leadership. Turning the board president into an owner is, therefore, one of your highest-stakes challenges as a superintendent. Here are some very practical steps that I've seen superintendents and other CEOs take to turn their board chairs into strong owners and stalwart partners:

- Reach a mutual understanding of the fundamental division of labor with your board president. Basically, the board president is responsible for leading the board's deliberations and for developing the board's leadership capacity, primarily through chairing the full board and the executive committee. The superintendent, as the district CEO, is responsible for all internal operations of the district and for supporting the board's deliberations. External relations—representing your district to the public at large and to key stakeholders—is shared turf that needs to be negotiated.
- Consciously divide the shared external agenda, looking for every opportunity to support your board president in playing the external leadership role successfully, for example, systematically coming up with speaking engagements for the president and making sure that he or she is well supported so the appearances are successful.
- Make every attempt to position your board president as the preeminent driver of the board's development as a governing body. Many board presidents come to the job, in my experience, without much knowledge about, or appetite for, developing the board's capacity to govern. So you might have to engage in some direct and/or indirect educational efforts, such as sharing pertinent articles and books and attending conference sessions on board leadership together. Your ultimate goal here is for your board president to come to view board development as a top priority and an area where he or she intends to leave a clear imprint.
- Do everything you can to make sure that your board president functions as a strong leader of the board's deliberations, including going out of your way to provide your president with privy briefing on major issues and—perhaps subtly—coaching your president on leadership style.

- Thoroughly understand your president in terms of his or her aspirations, motivations, likes and dislikes, personality, and skills so that you can ensure that the president's experience in leading the district and the board is as rich and personally rewarding as possible, thereby cementing your working partnership. If your president craves public exposure, you go out of your way to provide frequent speaking opportunities and to make sure that they go well. If your president's passion is the arts, you go out of your way to provide him or her opportunities to speak out on the subject at district forums and in district publications and to rub elbows with the arts faculty and students in appropriate settings. The point is, without toadying or violating leadership and management canons, you can care enough to provide your board president with a rich and rewarding experience during his or her term of office, and you will be rewarded with a stronger owner and partner to work with.

Key 5

Spice Up the Governing Stew

Main Message

Doing high-impact governing work is always demanding, but it can also be painful and even excruciatingly boring for board members as well. This need not be the case. Wearing the chief partnership officer hat (and taking on the roles of social director and theatrical producer as well), you, as your district's CEO, can—and should—help make the work of governing more inspiring, interesting, easier, and even fun for your board members. Fortunately, making governing a more attractive business doesn't have to be at the expense of the kind of high-impact leadership that your district requires in these challenging times, and it can be accomplished without violating canons of either sound management or good taste. Spicing up the governing stew for your board members is one of the most important strategies you can employ to turn them into close collaborators and solid partners.

Major Plot Lines

1. Beefing up the governing paycheck
2. Raising their sights
3. Making their governing work easier and more fun
4. Enriching their interpersonal experience

UPGRADING COMPENSATION

Appointments to the boards of major for-profit corporations are coveted, not only because such service is well remunerated, but also because the work tends to be carried out in a luxurious setting and is relatively stress-free, unless an Enron-like crisis erupts. I am reminded of an old friend of mine who, years ago, recounted the lavish accommodations, beautifully prepared and presented meals, and excellent brandy and cigars that made his quarterly corporate board meetings so pleasant. By contrast, almost all school board members, in common with other public/nonprofit trustees and directors, are expected to volunteer their time in the interest of the organization or institution they are governing and of the wider public good. Volunteering to participate in governing your school district is a concrete manifestation of the hallowed American tradition of paying back society for all of the benefits it has conferred on its more fortunate members.

Most school board members receive modest stipends for the substantial time they devote to governing and perhaps reimbursement for board-related expenses. Not only is the governing paycheck typically meager, the governing work of school board members can be a real grind—technically demanding, high pressure, and often somewhat boring. Your board very likely meets in a relatively spartan setting by corporate standards, board deliberations are often closely scrutinized by the media, and board members have been known to suffer verbal abuse from angry parents in the audience. Add to this the fact that many, if not most, board members receive a huge reading packet before every monthly meeting that typically makes for less-than-scintillating reading and you should not be surprised that so many school board members eventually become dispirited and that some burn out after only a few years of service.

As a board-savvy superintendent wearing your chief partnership officer hat, you don't have the option, realistically speaking, of substantially increasing your board members' monetary compensation. However, you can significantly beef up their nonmonetary paycheck if you devote serious time and attention to spicing up the governing stew by fashioning and executing strategies that will make their governing experience easier and more inspiring, interesting, and enjoyable.

RAISING THEIR SIGHTS

Experience has taught me that the great majority of school board members bring to their governing work both a sincere desire to make a real difference for the better in their district and a tremendous capacity for hard work. However, a few years of laboring in the governance trenches, even when the board is involved in providing truly high-impact governance that makes a real difference, can erode your board members' sense of mission and drain much of their enthusiasm and energy. During the past 20 years, I've read hundreds of pages of school board meeting minutes, so I know that the regular, month-by-month work of governing can be pretty deadly; in fact, I strongly recommend perusing board minutes as one of the most powerful antidotes to insomnia, as well as a deeply satisfying experience to any confirmed masochist.

One of the most important ways you can combat governing fatigue and reenergize your board members, giving them a new lease on their governing life, is to raise their sights above the day-to-day drudgery of governing. You can:

- inspire your board members by helping them see their governing work in the broader context of U.S. democratic and philanthropic traditions;
- excite their interest by drawing to their attention developments in the dynamic field of K–12 education and by sharing noteworthy experiences that are uniquely tied to your work as superintendent;
- ensure that board members are intensively involved at the open end of your district's "strategic funnel."

FOCUSING ON THE BROADER CONTEXT

One of Abraham Lincoln's goals—fully and beautifully achieved—in his address at Gettysburg was to raise people's sights above the carnage of that terrible battle, calling their attention to the fundamental U.S. principle—and context—of government "by, for and about the people." One of Franklin Roosevelt's goals in his immensely popular "fireside chats" during the Great Depression was to raise people's sights above the despair and fear caused by widespread unemployment, reminding them that

Americans are a resilient people who have nothing to fear but fear itself. Inspiring people by raising their sights, drawing their attention to fundamental principles and broader contexts, is one of the most important leadership roles of a CEO, no matter what the setting. This is certainly the case with school boards and their superintendents.

As a matter of fact, volunteering to govern a school district is a concrete manifestation of two powerful principles that provide a broad context for the work of your school board, and reminding board members of this context is a proven way to restore flagging spirits and provide valuable perspective on their governing activities. One principle, of course, is fundamentally democratic: that local school districts should be governed by representatives of the people residing in the district—elected directly or appointed by officials elected by the residents. School boards, then, play out the grand American experiment in self-government, and recognizing this solemnizes their work in a sense, elevating it above the often mundane work that boards must do.

In addition to embodying U.S. democratic principles, serving on school boards is also an expression of a powerful philanthropic principle that is uniquely American: that one can and should repay the society that has benefited him or her, by donating time and/or money to public causes. This principle animated John D. Rockefeller Jr. to give to nonprofit organizations fully half the estimated $1 billion fortune (perhaps $100 billion in today's dollars) that he inherited from his father, the founder of Standard Oil. It also motivated Bill Gates to endow the largest philanthropic foundation in human history. This philanthropic spirit animates people to give hundreds of hours to uncompensated service on the thousands of school boards around the country, along with an estimated 1.5 million other nonprofit and public governing bodies.

You can help keep your school board members' eyes on the fundamental principles undergirding their governing work and the broader context within which their work fits in a variety of simple, low-cost ways. For example, you can help ensure that the board's formal governing mission and the orientation for new board members both hark back to this broader context. You can also take advantage of presentations at ceremonial occasions, such as the annual district convocation, to remind board members that their governing activities are a practical expression of a proud democratic and philanthropic tradition that unites their boards with thousands of others around the country.

EXCITING THEIR INTEREST

K–12 education is a dynamic field experiencing constant change. Although it's hard to imagine a more exciting field in which to practice the art of governance, the excitement can get lost as board members slog through routine governing work meeting after meeting. You can certainly spice up the governing stew for your board members by calling their attention to the exciting issues that abound in the wider world of education—related to educational performance standards and accountability, choice and the allocation of public dollars to nonpublic educational alternatives to our school systems, the role of public schools in teaching "values" and the determination of whose values to teach, the social responsibilities of our schools in dealing with the ramifications of nontraditional families, and many more. You can also make sure that your board members are well briefed on changing educational technologies and methodologies, the ramifications of new federal and state legislation and regulations, and the implications of pending legislation.

Experience has taught me that most, if not all, of your board members are likely to be an avid audience for briefings on the nonroutine activities that you engage in as their CEO, such as your service on other boards in the community, your meetings with community leaders, your involvement in state and national association work, your speaking engagements, and the like. Making an effort to fill them in on the more exciting aspects of your CEO work, in person and via fax and e-mail, says that you really are concerned about the quality of their governing experience.

THE STRATEGIC FUNNEL

Strategic planning is the gold standard for board participation in the affairs of your school district, not only because of the stakes involved in dealing with strategic issues, but also because board members are uniquely qualified to contribute at what I call the open end of the "strategic funnel"—where your district's vision and values are revisited, environmental conditions and trends are reviewed, the strategic issues facing your district are identified, and possible change initiatives to deal with the issues are brainstormed. No other process is so effective, in my experience, at raising your board members' sights above the routine drudgery of governing, capturing their imagination, and rekindling their enthusiasm.

An annual strategic work session or retreat, kicking off your district's annual planning process, is a surefire way to involve your board productively at the open end of the strategic funnel. You can ensure that this annual event is both highly productive in terms of planning output and thoroughly enjoyable for your board members by taking two important steps:

- Ensuring that your board members are involved in both preparing for and leading the retreat. For example, your board's planning committee might present a trends and conditions briefing to kick off the retreat, using slides that you and your executive team have helped develop, and board members might lead breakout groups, dealing with such matters as updating your district's vision and identifying educational issues.
- Avoiding any attempt to reach formal consensus or make firm decisions during the retreat, relying instead on a well-defined follow-up process for the purpose of decision making subsequent to the retreat. By resisting the temptation to get every loose end tied up in only a day or two together, you can ensure that people will be more relaxed and better able to engage in the kind of creative, open-minded dialogue that is essential for truly high-quality strategic planning.

MAKING THE WORK EASIER AND MORE FUN

Governing your school district is a serious business, but you can take some simple, very practical steps to make the work less painful and more enjoyable for your board members. One of the most important is to ensure that the reports and recommendations that are sent to the board in the regular meeting packet are designed for easy reading and understanding. This can be one of the top goals of the board's standing committees. For example, I recently sat in on a meeting of a board's performance monitoring committee, at which the format and content of the monthly financial report were thoroughly discussed, with an eye to making the financial report more user-friendly. Board members had been receiving a multipage financial report chock full of numbers that was extremely difficult to understand and ugly to boot.

It didn't take long for committee members to reach agreement with the superintendent on the design of an executive summary that, using bar charts, would compare actual with budgeted expenditures—year-to-date and for the month—by major programmatic and administrative categories. Since some board members felt uncomfortable giving up the detail that they were accustomed to receiving, it was agreed to provide it in an appendix to the report. You can also make the work of your board easier by ensuring that complex reports and major recommendations are transmitted with a cover sheet that provides an executive summary, highlighting the recommended actions and the associated costs.

Superintendents who are willing to don the theatrical producer hat can put their minds to making the governing experience of their board members more enjoyable. One of the most effective ways, which I discussed in the last chapter, is to book your board members for speaking engagements in such forums as Rotary and Lions clubs, just as long as you make sure they are supported in taking on this public relations work (for example, slides to use, materials to hand out, an opportunity to rehearse). Speaking can be an interesting and ego-satisfying experience for board members, as can representing your district on ad hoc community task forces and committees. For example, one school board member I know recently represented the public school system on her city's economic development task force, which over a period of eight months fashioned recommendations for attracting new business to the city by various means, including featuring the public schools in promotional material. This was more than merely an "extracurricular" experience intended to enrich the governing life of a board member, as it turns out, because one of the direct results of the task force's work was wide agreement to support a tax increase for the school system.

Board meetings themselves can be spiced up to make the governing experience more enjoyable and interesting. For example, one school district I know regularly rotates school board meetings among the different school buildings in the district, making a point to invite parents of children enrolled in the buildings to attend the meetings and conducting a tour of the buildings before convening the board meetings. Another district I know has built a "Spotlight on the Faculty" section into its regular monthly board meeting agenda. Managed by the board's planning and development committee, the spotlight segment has added spice to board meetings by featuring outstanding faculty members, who describe their work and respond to board member questions. Another district employs a similar approach, but includes students as well as faculty. And providing board members with opportunities to observe classes in different buildings is another way to add spice to the governing experience.

THE TIES THAT BIND

Narrowing the distance that separates people, breaking through unnecessary barriers, making human connections: these are important ways to enrich your board members' governing experience and to strengthen your partnership with the board. Board-savvy superintendents well know that familiarity breeds not contempt, but the mutual understanding and emotional bonding that help cement teamwork and partnership: among board members, between the board and superintendent, and between the board and executive team. Knowing someone at a deeper level builds a kind of emotional line of credit that can be drawn on when grappling with thorny issues and dealing with the inevitable stresses and strains involved in high-impact governing.

However, over the years I've seen many CEOs, including a number of superintendents, make the mistake of keeping their board members at a distance by overrelying on formal communication and avoiding more personal interaction. And these formalists often compound the error by keeping their executive team members away from regular, intensive interaction with the board. As far as I can tell, a superintendent who maintains an overly formal, unnecessarily distant relationship with his or her board is usually captive to a defensive mindset, seeing the board as a damage control challenge rather than as a creative partnership-building challenge. Whatever the reasons, maintaining unnecessary interpersonal barriers is one sure way to weaken the board–superintendent working relationship over time.

As a board-savvy superintendent, you will want to take advantage of every opportunity to break down interpersonal barriers and strengthen the emotional ties that bind board members more closely and you and your executives to the board. I have seen board-savvy superintendents successfully employ a variety of practical, low-cost techniques over the years. For example, you can adopt a schedule of regular one-on-one meetings with your board members, perhaps over lunch or breakfast either monthly or bi-monthly, depending on the size of your board. One-on-one interaction is the most effective way to ensure that you are in touch with the real—as opposed to public—opinions and feelings of your board members. You can also take the initiative in orchestrating and facilitating social interaction involving the board as a whole along with you and your executive team—for example, some of the more common approaches include an informal get-together over lunch or a light supper before the monthly board meeting; periodic receptions, perhaps cohosted by you and the board president; a December holiday party; a summer picnic featuring the annual board–staff softball game; a social evening built into the annual strategic work session kicking off the planning cycle.

And you should keep in mind that standing committees, as I have discussed earlier, provide an ideal venue for in-depth board–superintendent–executive team interaction that is free of much of the formality of the regular monthly board meeting.

Key 6

Get Your Senior
Administrators on Board

The Main Message

The senior administrators who make up the executive team of your district are critical participants in building and maintaining the board–superintendent partnership. The more strongly committed they are to your governing principles, the more knowledgeable they are about the business of governing, and the more actively involved they are in working as a team with you on board-related matters, the stronger your partnership with your board is likely to be.

Major Plot Lines

1. Turning your executives into effective governing partners
2. Making powerful use of standing committees
3. Keeping your board high on the executive team agenda
4. Adhering to the principle of collective ownership

PARTNERING WITH THE EXECUTIVE TEAM

Every board-savvy superintendent knows that the preeminent key to a strong, productive, and enduring board–superintendent partnership is the board's proactive and creative involvement in generating the kind of high-impact governing that makes a real difference in the affairs of the district. All board-savvy superintendents also know that their board's successful involvement in high-impact governing depends on strong, continuous executive planning and support, which no superintendent could possibly provide alone. The senior administrators making up your district's executive team must, therefore, be active partners with you, as superintendent, in supporting the board's governing work if you want to build and maintain a productive, positive, and enduring partnership with your board. To function as effective partners with you in supporting the board, your executives must first understand and fully buy into your governing philosophy, and, second, they must become true experts in the governing business.

Unless your executive team is already working hand in glove with you in supporting your board's governing work, turning your executive team members into strong partners in working with your school board is likely to involve much more than just issuing marching orders. Executives who have recently joined your team are likely to have had only minimal contact with the board, and that interaction has probably been relatively formal and at arm's length. Even longer-tenured team members may have acquired only a superficial knowledge of the governing field, and some of them are likely to have become wedded to principles and behaviors that will conflict with your partnership-building strategies. Working with a recently appointed superintendent a few years ago, I learned a valuable lesson about the importance of the CEO making sure that executives are firmly grounded in the CEO's philosophy and methodologies relative to working with the board.

A CASE OF INADEQUATE EDUCATION

This new superintendent inherited an executive team, most of whose members had spent several years working with her predecessor, who was a virtuoso of the old school: control-oriented where the board was concerned and highly skilled at the "good old boy" type of interpersonal relations. He had spent considerable time over the years schmoozing with individual board members and had kept board members busy reading well-crafted staff-produced documents. After 10 years in the job, this master of board manipulation was finally forced to resign when the frustrated young turks on the board became a majority. During the selection process, the school board made sure that the new superintendent was strongly committed to higher-impact board leadership and to a real partnership with the board. However, translating this commitment into action at the executive level turned out to be a daunting challenge for the new superintendent, primarily because of a knowledge deficit and philosophical disconnect among executive team members.

The first significant test came early in the new superintendent's tenure, when she—armed with a firm mandate from her board—began to work with the executive team on the design of a new strategic planning process that would involve the board early in providing direction, rather than merely responding, to staff-prepared planning documentation. The superintendent appointed 3 senior team members to serve on a task force whose charge was to fashion the new design and present it to the executive team for in-depth review in 10 weeks. Expecting this to be a relatively straightforward task, the superintendent spent an hour with the task force at its first meeting, emphasizing the need for a more creative, substantive role for the board, and then left them alone to map out the strategic planning design. When the task force presented its design recommendations, the superintendent understood full well that she had not prepared the task force adequately for its work, and back to the drawing board the group went, with a fuller understanding this time of the philosophical framework for their work.

The original strategic planning design that the task force presented reflected a deeply ingrained executive commitment to finished staff work. Every member of the executive team had had drummed into his or her head by the former superintendent the principle that anything going to the board was to be beautifully crafted and basically finished. Options might be discussed, but there was always a staff recommendation based on thorough formal analysis. The prior strategic plan, for example, had been largely prepared by a consulting firm with ample executive team input but virtually no board involvement until the review-and-comment stage of the process. Therefore, rather than paying adequate attention to practical ways for involving the board early in the planning process (at the open end of the "strategic funnel"), the task force concentrated in its initial design effort on making the finished plan that would be presented to the board a higher-quality, more comprehensive document reflecting more rigorous information collection and analysis on the part of administrative staff. Indeed, although they recommended sensible enhancements, the task force really did miss the main point.

EDUCATING THE TEAM

The first step in getting your executive team on board as active partners in supporting high-impact governing in your district is to make sure all team members are thoroughly grounded in your governing philosophy. This requires that you articulate—clearly and in detail—the fundamental values and principles that you hold dear, and expect adherence to, in the governing arena, and that you also take the time to explore with your executives the practical application of your philosophy in working with the board. If you concur with the 8 keys that are described in this book, for example, your governance philosophy will include a strong belief in and commitment to:

- a board that generates truly high-impact governance that makes a real difference in your district;
- a board that is proactively and creatively involved in making critical governing decisions, not merely reacting to finished staff work;
- a partnership between the board and its superintendent that is close, positive, and productive;
- full utilization of board members' experience, talents, knowledge, and community connections in the governing process;
- frequent, close interaction between the board and executive team.

Of course, agreement at the level of values and principles is only part of the educational process required to turn your executive team members into full partners in supporting the board's governing work. They also need a thorough grounding in the mechanics of the governing process, starting with a clear definition of what governing means and moving on to the nuts and bolts involved in doing governing work, such as the board's role in strategic planning, budget preparation, performance monitoring and the like, the use of committees as a governing tool, and practical ways to provide board members with a more ego-satisfying governing experience.

The most powerful learning always takes place on the job, as your executive team members participate—collectively and individually—in supporting the governing process, under your close direction (remember, the board is your unique "program" as CEO; you would never want to delegate its direction to anyone, no matter how senior). You can also build a high-quality governance library, making sure that your executives are exposed to pertinent publications in the field. Carefully selected educational workshops can also be useful. In this regard, one superintendent I know actually put together her own daylong workshop on public/nonprofit governance, which she annually presents to executives and senior administrators who have not yet participated.

THOSE GOVERNING ENGINES AGAIN

I have paid quite a bit of attention to standing committees in earlier chapters for the simple reason that they are one of the primary mechanisms for ensuring that your school board functions as a truly high-impact governing body. They are also a very effective mechanism for involving your executive team members actively in supporting the board's governing work—in a less formal setting, away from the close public scrutiny that attends full board meetings, with far more opportunity for give and take and on-the-job learning. You will recall from earlier discussion that committees must be well designed if they are to serve as effective governing tools, corresponding to the broad streams within which governing decisions are made about governing "products" (planning and performance oversight being the preeminent streams), rather than being tied to narrow programmatic or administrative silos.

In my experience, the key to effective executive team support of your board's standing committees is the designation of an executive team member to serve as chief staff to each standing committee, in this capacity heading a support team of executives and senior administrators, whose membership will vary with the particular matters being dealt with by each committee. For example, it would make good sense for a district's chief financial officer to serve as chief staff to the board's performance oversight committee, in light of that committee's responsibility for reviewing financial performance. The core team members for the performance oversight committee, who never change, might include the district controller, director of administrative services, and management information services director. However, when the committee is taking an in-depth look at a particular educational program, you would want your executive in charge of curriculum and instruction, perhaps along with one or more other instructional staff, to be involved on the committee's support team.

Designating a member of your executive team to serve as chief staff to each committee builds in accountability at the executive level, in effect identifying a person whose professional success is publicly tied to the effectiveness of the standing committee, rather than you, as superintendent, being the only officer clearly accountable for committee performance. In his or her capacity of chief staff to a standing committee, the executive team member should take accountability for:

• working closely with the board member chairing the committee in developing future committee agendas;
• directly supporting the committee chair in carrying out his or her leadership role (for example, traipsing over to the office of the planning committee chair a couple of weeks before the next committee meeting to provide her with a thorough briefing on a complex issue to be dealt with);
• playing a quality control role, working with the other members of the committee support team to make sure that all items being sent to the committee are not only complete and accurate, but also that they arrive in enough time for careful review by committee members.

Serving as chief staff and team leader for one of your board's standing committees is a demanding responsibility, both because of the complexity and importance of governing work and the complex relationships involved. In essence, executives serving as chief committee staff are accountable not only to the superintendent as CEO, but also to the committee chair and the whole executive team. Although the chief staff will obviously want to keep the superintendent apprised of any dealings with his or her committee chair, he or she will necessarily spend considerable time in one-on-one meetings with the chair, requiring a high level of trust on the superintendent's part. Experience has taught me that one of the most reliable ways to avert problems is for the superintendent to meet regularly with each member of the chief committee staff, reviewing their work with their committee chairs and providing guidance, as appropriate, on issues to be discussed with the chairs.

MAKING GOOD USE OF THE EXECUTIVE TEAM

Board-savvy superintendents always use their executive teams as powerful vehicles for planning, managing, and coordinating the superintendent's board governing "program." Experience has taught that this works best when the executive team, with the superintendent in the chair, meets once monthly for 2 to 3 hours solely for the purpose of dealing with school board matters. In this capacity, the executive team is uniquely qualified to play 3 important roles for the superintendent:

1. Assist the superintendent in board-capacity building. The regular executive team meeting devoted to governing matters is an ideal venue for discussion of the superintendent's targets and strategies for building the board–superintendent–executive team working partnership: what progress is being made, what problems have cropped up and how they might be dealt with, how particular executive team members might assist in carrying out the partnership-building strategies, and what new targets should be set.
2. Provide support for chief staff heading committee support teams. The executive team members serving as chief committee staff can bring to the executive team special staff support needs that require the support of other executives. To take a recent real-life example, I was working with a district whose executive team leader for the planning committee was in the process of developing a comprehensive conditions and trends briefing, which the planning committee would present, using PowerPoint slides, at the annual strategic planning retreat 11 weeks later. The data required for the presentation, relative to both internal district performance and the external environment, could not have been gathered by the core members of the planning committee team alone, so the matter was brought to the executive team. At the meeting, the associate superintendent for administrative services agreed to lend the planning committee team two of her staff for an estimated 20 hours to compile the needed data.

3. Exercise quality control. In light of the stakes involved in supporting your school board's governing work, you will want to have your executive team review and sign off on all documentation being sent to standing committees, making sure that the material is well crafted, complete, and accurate. And the executive team can serve as an ideal vehicle for critiquing important presentations being made either to a standing committee or the full board. Take the example of the conditions and trends briefing being developed for the planning committee. After the data have been assembled and the PowerPoint slides put together, the planning committee's support team can do a dry run of the presentation with the executive team, for the purpose of having team members' best thinking on the quality of both the content and format of the presentation. The executive team can also anticipate questions that might be raised by the data, giving support team members a chance to practice their responses.

THE PRINCIPLE OF COLLECTIVE OWNERSHIP

Your district's executive team can be a truly effective vehicle for supporting your board's high-impact governing if the superintendent and all team members abide by the principle of collective ownership of the governing "program." The executive team's collective ownership of the governing function does not reduce the accountability of the chief staff to the committees for ensuring high-quality staff support for committee work. Rather, collective ownership means that the executives serving as chief committee staff are accountable to their peers on the executive team and cannot bypass them in working with the committees.

Executive team collective ownership is a must for two reasons. First, governing work is so complex and high-stakes that it deserves the best thinking of everyone on the executive team. Second, the professional success of every executive on the team is closely tied to the health of the board–superintendent–executive team partnership, and so, from an ethical perspective, executive team members should be invited to comment on strategies for working with the board and its standing committees and on the quality of all materials being sent to the committees and full board.

Key 7

Keep Expectations in Sync

The Main Message

One of the most important ways to make sure that the board–superintendent partnership starts off on the right foot and remains positive and productive is to negotiate—and periodically renegotiate—superintendent performance targets and to regularly assess superintendent performance against these targets. Leaving performance expectations unclear is a risky course of action that has disrupted many a superintendent's career.

Major Plot Lines

1. Moving beyond distance
2. Paying the price of benign neglect
3. Establishing accountability
4. Negotiating performance targets
5. Evaluating performance

LET YOUR BOARD GET IN YOUR HAIR

Over and over through the years, superintendents and other CEOs have said to me that they are worried about their board "looking over their shoulder" and are on guard against their board "getting in their hair." "Let me do my executive job," they say, "and let the board do its work, and let's stay out of each other's way." As I hope this book has thus far made clear, although there are board members out there who occasionally need a slap on the wrist for meddling in executive or even administrative matters, there is a far greater danger in allowing too much distance to develop between you and your board—in not working closely enough together. In real life rather than abstract theory, much of the board–superintendent partnership is actually played out in the gray area between the poles of "pure" administration and "pure" governance. In earlier chapters, I have discussed how superintendents, playing their CEO role to the hilt, must be actively involved in developing their boards' governing capacity and in helping their boards to govern. Distance is, indeed, an overrated virtue in the governing business.

A good starting point for any superintendent aspiring to build a close, enduring, and productive partnership with the board is to acknowledge that effective CEOship of your school district *is* a valid board concern— indeed, one of its highest priorities. Rather than guard against board involvement in defining the superintendent's role as CEO of the district, the board-savvy superintendent will both welcome and facilitate board involvement—from the very get-go, even during the negotiation stage before the board has finalized the appointment of the superintendent. Once you are on board as a superintendent, there are 4 principal steps that can be taken to make sure that you and your board are in agreement as to your CEO leadership role:

1. The board assigns accountability for managing the board–superintendent working relationship to a particular standing committee.
2. The accountable committee and superintendent annually reach agreement on the specific leadership challenges that deserve special superintendent attention, the superintendent's specific performance targets, and any special board support that might be needed to assure superintendent success in meeting these targets.
3. The board, at least annually, conducts an in-depth assessment of superintendent performance against these targets and reaches agreement with the superintendent on corrective actions that need to be taken to bring performance up to standard in particular areas.
4. The board and superintendent hold one or more interim, less-intensive assessment sessions during the year, renegotiating targets as changing circumstances dictate.

Ensuring that this kind of rigorous, systematic "CEO performance management system" is fully implemented is not an abstract "good government" concern; it is one of the preeminent keys to a sound, mutually satisfying board–superintendent partnership and to your ultimate success as CEO. Not moving aggressively on this front would be a surefire strategy for jeopardizing your career.

A TALE OF WOE

Allow me to recount a true story that, with variations, I have seen played out in various settings over the years. The names have been changed, but this sad tale is not fiction:

The Woodhaven Consolidated School District Board knew exactly what it needed in a new superintendent, and it got what it wanted in Dr. Joan Wentworth. The district's relations with the public at large in Woodhaven were terribly frayed—witness the loss of two crucial tax issues over the past year, which has led to the elimination of the theater arts program and some faculty and administrative layoffs. And there was a state of near-warfare between the district and both the city government and chamber of commerce, which had on several occasions found the district standoffish and unresponsive when approached to collaborate in economic renewal initiatives in Woodhaven. The board knew that it needed above all a consummate diplomat who could lead the district in reaching out to key constituencies in Woodhaven. Joan Wentworth was a superb choice, with her commanding stage presence, successful experience in public speaking, highly accessible style, and obvious passion for partnership building beyond the district's internal boundaries.

Joan did exactly what the board wanted: frayed relationships were repaired; enough community support was built to pass 2 desperately needed tax issues, including one for capital improvements; and the Woodhaven District was actively engaged in a number of key community development initiatives. But 3 years after bringing Joan to the district, the board was becoming increasingly dissatisfied with her as CEO, and a couple of board members were lobbying their colleagues to not renew Joan's contract the next year. In a nutshell, Joan's performance, while superb on the diplomatic front, dealing with the public and key stakeholders, was far less impressive in the administrative area, which was an increasing concern of several, perhaps a majority of, board members. On a number of occasions, board members had complained about the process for developing the annual budget and the format in which it was presented, which was confusing to virtually everyone on the board. And Joan didn't seem at all responsive when she was encouraged at more than one performance-monitoring committee meeting to undertake a renovation of the vendor contracting and payment system, which was outmoded and terribly inefficient. It clearly "wasn't her thing," and occasional complaints and pressure were not getting anywhere. The glow in this working partnership had worn off.

How does the story end? Sad to say, in this case, Joan's contract was not renewed, and she left the Woodhaven District after 3 years. This is a classic story and an all-too-common ending in the world of boards and their CEOs in both the for-profit and the public/nonprofit sectors, but it need not have ended unhappily. All CEOs, including school superintendents, are brought into organizations under particular circumstances, and very often the marching orders are quite clear: clean up the shop, rebuild image and public relations, get a tax issue passed, deal with low morale, improve performance in particular lagging buildings, and so on. Of course, the original circumstances change over time, which means that a board's expectations for superintendent leadership evolve; this is a normal situation that need not be the slippery slope to a fatal break in the board–CEO relationship. A well-designed, rigorously executed performance evaluation process is the most important way to keep the relationship on track.

PINPOINTING BOARD ACCOUNTABILITY

A key first step is to designate a particular board standing committee as responsible for maintenance of the board–superintendent partnership, including negotiating superintendent performance targets and assessing performance. This is the surest way to make sure that this extremely important matter commands the time and close attention that it deserves. Leaving it in the hands of the board as a whole has proved to be an unwieldy and ineffective approach, and delegating it to the board president/chair would be beyond the pale, putting far too much responsibility in the hands of a single board member, while also narrowing board ownership of the relationship and exposing the superintendent to inordinate political risk.

Experience has taught that delegating responsibility to the executive (or governance) committee, chaired by the board president and consisting of other standing committee chairs, makes good sense. Not only does this ensure the involvement of the board president, but it also involves the heads of committees that work closely and continuously with the superintendent. By the way, delegating responsibility to a particular committee does not mean that other board members are excluded from the process of setting superintendent targets and assessing performance. What it does mean is that a committee will take responsibility for designing the process and overseeing its execution.

SETTING PERFORMANCE TARGETS

The purpose of setting specific targets for superintendent performance is to give both partners in the relationship a reasonably objective yardstick for measuring performance. Without targets, performance assessment is inevitably less meaningful and dangerously subjective, as is the case with the checklist approach that some boards still employ, which measures broad functional competence (for example, on a 5-degree scale, how well does our superintendent perform in public representation of the district, in long-range financial planning, in financial management, in providing educational leadership, and so on?). Assessing performance in functional categories allows for an unacceptable level of subjectivity, exposing the superintendent unfairly to judgments that have more to do with style and politics than performance. What a school board should care about is accomplishment, not functional competence.

Keep in mind that superintendent performance targets can be set at 2 levels, both of which are essential for sound performance assessment and relationship maintenance: (1) overall district performance targets that are typically set through the annual operational planning/budget preparation process; and (2) the superintendent's CEO-specific leadership targets, reflecting leadership priorities and governing the allocation of superintendent time. Without question, as CEO of the whole district, the superintendent is always accountable for district performance overall—educationally, financially, administratively. The superintendent is accountable to the school board for revenues and expenditures meeting planned targets—monthly,

quarterly, annually; for planned improvements in state test scores, graduation, and dropout rates; for planned efficiencies from implementing the contracting process, and the like. If districtwide performance lags significantly
in any area, the board has the right and responsibility to ask the superintendent for an explanation and to take this into account in evaluating superintendent performance.

What you should not forget, however, is that superintendent performance targets that are CEO-specific are just as important as districtwide
performance standards in maintaining a healthy board–superintendent
partnership. In fact, failing to reach agreement on CEO-specific targets is,
in my experience, one of the most important reasons that board–superintendent partnerships crash and burn. Some CEOs, including superintendents, might feel threatened by the prospect of negotiating their CEO leadership priorities and the allocation of their CEO time with their board,
probably because talking with the board about how they use their time
seems to deal with the *how,* not the *what,* of their leadership role. However, agreement at the more general, districtwide level will fail to get to
the heart of superintendent performance, leaving the superintendent vulnerable to board members' subjective judgment. The magic of effective
performance assessment is in the details.

Based on experience, I recommend that superintendent-specific CEO
leadership targets be set in a two-step process. First, the board and superintendent should reach agreement on what appear to be the preeminent
leadership challenges that merit significant individual attention from the
superintendent. This can be most effectively done by dividing the CEO
job into its major categories:

- The board–CEO relationship, including CEO support for the board
- Educational leadership
- Administrative and financial leadership
- External relations leadership
- Superintendent professional development

For example, the board and superintendent might agree that among the
most important challenges facing the district are (a) considerable dissatisfaction among board members about their governing role, which is too
vaguely defined (falling in the board–CEO relationship category); (b) a

federal mandate that students be allowed to transfer from failing schools (educational leadership); (c) a projected significant revenue shortfall 2 years out (financial leadership); and (d) constant negative attention in the media (external relations).

These CEO leadership challenges might be brainstormed in a board–superintendent work session, after which they are refined by the executive committee and superintendent. Or the superintendent might take a preliminary cut, then review and discuss it with the executive committee. The point is to make sure that more detailed superintendent leadership targets are actually developed in the context of—and driven by—what appear to be the most serious challenges calling for superintendent time and attention.

Having reached agreement on the leadership challenges, the executive committee and superintendent can now turn to the more specific superintendent leadership targets that are intended to deal with the agreed-upon challenges. The question the executive committee asks the superintendent is, "What do you intend to accomplish, as CEO of our district, to make progress in dealing with each of the leadership challenges that we have agreed you should focus on?" There is a second question that the school board must ask, however, if the process is to be fully fair to the superintendent: "In order to achieve each of these targets, what special support do you anticipate needing from us as your board?"

For example, with regard to the federally mandated process for student transfer from failing schools, the superintendent's target might be submission to the school board, by a certain time, of a detailed strategy for meeting the mandate. With regard to the anticipated revenue shortfall, the superintendent might promise to appoint an advisory committee involving outside experts as well as selected administrators to fashion a plan for review by the board's performance oversight committee this coming October. With regard to the negative media attention, the superintendent might commit to 2 targets: putting a formal public relations office into operation within 6 months and spending approximately a quarter of her time in the community affairs arena to raise the district's image in the community.

I strongly recommend, based on experience, that the superintendent develop a list of proposed targets for discussion and finalization with the executive committee, rather than having the committee and superintendent attempt to come up with a list from scratch in a work session. In developing the list, the superintendent should also identify specific board support requirements and commitments that will be needed to meet the targets. For example, in order to spend significant time in the community arena, personally burnishing the district's image and rebuilding relationships with particular high-priority stakeholders such as the office of the mayor, the superintendent might need the support of a strong public relations professional to head a new district office, requiring that $230,000 be budgeted from reserves. For the superintendent to succeed in helping the board clarify its governing role, the board might need to set aside 2 days this coming summer for an intensive retreat and approve a budget for professional facilitation.

These superintendent CEO-specific performance targets will not, for the most part, be scientifically measurable, but they will make up a highly relevant framework for assessing superintendent performance. I want to caution, however, that the targets will be only as relevant as the time and attention paid to developing them. At the very least, in my experience, the executive committee should commit to 3 to 4 intensive work sessions lasting between 2 and 4 hours each—1 or 2 sessions to reach agreement on the superintendent leadership challenges and 2 sessions to finalize performance targets. In light of the stakes involved for your district, not committing the requisite time to this process would amount to dereliction of duty as a governing board.

ASSESSING PERFORMANCE

The magic of effective board assessment of superintendent performance lies in the formulation of the CEO-specific performance targets, not in the evaluation itself. The challenge is to make sure that superintendent performance is actually measured against these targets and not based on more subjective, functional measures (the "How good is he at. . . ?" approach). You might consider building the following features, in addition to negotiated performance targets, into your district's superintendent evaluation process to ensure that it realizes its full promise in terms of the board–superintendent working partnership:

- Conduct the in-depth evaluation of superintendent performance annually.

- Hold interim, less-intensive assessment sessions semiannually, or even quarterly, providing an opportunity to adjust performance targets to changing district circumstances.
- Meticulously prepare for the evaluation session. In my experience, it makes good sense for committee members and the superintendent to individually assess performance—in writing—against the targets that have been set before sitting down together to discuss the results. This pre-assessment activity should focus on identifying performance shortfalls, analyzing possible reasons for the underperformance, and proposing possible actions to bring performance up to snuff.
- Hold an intensive face-to-face session involving the committee and superintendent, at which the individual assessments are discussed and consensus is reached. There is no valid argument for the committee to meet without the superintendent present; not only would such a meeting be disrespectful to the superintendent, it would also lack the superintendent's very pertinent input into the assessment process.
- Hold a session involving the superintendent and other board members, at which the committee reviews the evaluation results and responds to board members' questions.
- Conduct a final session at which the superintendent presents a plan for dealing with each of the identified performance problems during the coming year. This final session might also kick off the process of reaching agreement on new performance targets for the new year.

Key 8

Stay on the High-Growth Path

The Main Message

Continuous change is a staple in the life of all organizations, including school districts, and in all relationships, including the board–superintendent partnership. Maintaining a close and productive board–superintendent partnership depends on the superintendent's growth—and change—in response to advances in the field of public/nonprofit governance and related fields and to the changing cast of characters on the board.

Major Plot Lines

1. Keeping up with advances in governance and related fields
2. Adapting to the changing cast

CONTINUING TO GROW AS A GOVERNANCE EXPERT

These are exciting times in the mother field of public/nonprofit leadership and management, within which public school administration fits. Three closely related—indeed, inextricably entwined—areas that are pertinent to school leaders are going through dramatic change: new concepts, new methodologies, and a growing literature:

- Board leadership: moving from the old-time passive-reactive board to boards that are proactively involved in producing really high-impact

67

governing decisions that make a significant difference in the affairs of
their organizations
- CEO leadership: moving from the command-and-control tradition to a
  more contemporary mix of organizational architect, designer, and facilitator
- Strategic planning: moving from old-fashioned, comprehensive, long-
  range planning of the 3- or 5-year ilk to a focus on addressing strategic
  issues and generating significant innovation and change

Maintaining a close and productive partnership with your board requires that you stay abreast of developments in all 3 of these critical areas. At the top of the list is governance itself, of course, and you will want
to take advantage of new techniques for strengthening your board's capacity to govern, rather than relying on mere inheritance of past practices.
And the area of strategic planning is extraordinarily important to building
an enduring partnership with your board. As I discussed earlier in this
book, playing a proactive, leading role in making strategic decisions is the
"gold standard" for board involvement in your school district. Strategic
planning as a logic, a set of concepts, and a methodology is being dra-
matically rethought as this book is being written. One of your key responsibilities as superintendent is to make sure that the most recent thinking on strategic planning (to the extent that it is based on thorough testing,
of course) is taken into account in designing a strategic planning process
for your school district, including spelling out the role of the school board
in the process.

Unless you keep up with developments in the areas of governance,
strategic planning, and CEOship—continuously updating your knowledge
and expertise—you will be dangerously vulnerable to the sales pitches of
consultants peddling their pet approaches. It is easy to see how your working partnership with your board might be damaged by their spending several months implementing a "governance model" that focuses on keeping
the board in line and out of administrative affairs without providing for a
creative role in shaping major decisions, or by your board going through
a strategic planning process that, ultimately, ended up making very little
difference in district operations.

In light of your undoubtedly hectic schedule, with plenty yet to do at
the end of every work day, you obviously cannot carry on a continuous re-

search effort aimed at keeping you up-to-date in all 3 of these critical areas. However, you can ask someone on your staff to take responsibility for building and maintaining a library of periodicals and books that you should be looking over when you can find time. As a first step, your staff person will need to do a small research project, identifying the publishers with a major presence in public/nonprofit leadership and management and making sure that your office is on their mailing list for catalogues and special promotions. You will also want to know what periodicals are likely to provide you with insightful and current information on governance, strategic planning, and CEOship. If feasible, you might have your staff person regularly screen articles and books, directing your attention to the ones most deserving of your time and perhaps even producing summaries of articles and chapters.

Of course, the publications catalogues of the national associations in your field, such as the American Association of School Administrators and the National School Boards Association, are an obvious source of pertinent publications, but you will want to make sure in building your library that you go beyond the field of public education, tapping into work going on in the broader field of public/nonprofit leadership and management. In this regard, for example, you might consider joining Board-Source (formerly the National Center for Nonprofit Boards). Works on governance, strategic planning, and CEOship in the for-profit sector are often pertinent to public education leadership; for example, the *Harvard Business Review* is a highly regarded resource for leaders in all sectors. And you are well advised to go beyond the field of management in looking for information and inspiration. In my work, for example, I have found that a well-researched biography can be a powerful source of wisdom on CEO leadership.

You might also have your in-house librarian take responsibility for identifying high-level educational opportunities that you might take advantage of when you can find the time. The most obvious source will be the annual conferences of the state and national associations you belong to, but you might also keep your eye out for pertinent educational offerings at nearby colleges and universities, especially their schools of education, public affairs, and nonprofit management. Many institutions these days offer half- and full-day executive-level workshops on topics such as nonprofit governance, and if you are a discerning consumer, you can significantly enhance your knowledge and expertise at a reasonable cost in time and money.

Mentoring is an often neglected educational tool that is well worth considering. Learning from more experienced colleagues who have demonstrated notable success in working with their boards is the first thing that will come to mind, but you do not want to neglect board members as possible mentors. Although you might have to overcome a bit of ego resistance (Do I really want any of my board members to see me as their student?), the fact is that many board members bring a wealth of knowledge and experience to subjects such as CEOship, governance, and strategic planning. They do not have to know that they are mentoring you, but by consulting board members on particular issues, asking the right questions, and listening carefully, you can be mentored. My experience is that board members in general want to be helpful to their superintendent, appreciate being asked for counsel, and tend to be more closely tied emotionally to superintendents who ask for their best thinking on a topic. Not long ago, I saw a superintendent benefit tremendously from the mentoring of a wise corporate CEO on his school board, who drew on deep experience in counseling the superintendent on executive team-building techniques.

ADAPTING TO THE CHANGING CAST

Growing in the governance business also means learning to adapt to the changing cast of characters on your board over the years. Of course, if you are around long enough, you will see whole boards turning over more than once, and you will be faced with the never-ending challenge of adapting to new styles, new expectations, new experiences, new skills, and new capacities. What is most critical, in my experience, is your paying close attention to the broader social and cultural change that shapes the expectations and behavior of your board members and might, as you adapt your style of communication and interaction, force you out of your comfort zone. Here are some sweeping changes that I have seen in working with boards around the country in recent years:

- Demand for immediate impact: Board members these days tend not to have the patience to go through a lengthy period of getting up to speed and learning the governing ropes. They expect to hit the ground running, making a real difference soon after joining the board, and so they will not put up with a poorly defined governing role or an ill-defined committee structure that produces little impact. A board-savvy superintendent will, therefore, make sure that the board's governing design is systematically updated, even if some board members have to be dragged kicking and screaming to the drawing board.

- Tremendous time pressure: The kind of people who populate school boards have always been busier than average, but the accelerating pace of life these days has made volunteering to serve on boards an increasingly stressful activity. Board members now typically expect their governing time to be efficiently planned and managed, meaning that the board-savvy superintendent will pay close attention to employing techniques that economize on board members' time. For example, board members will be wired for e-mail communication; committee meetings will be held via teleconference; audio/visual aids will be employed to get the substance of reports across faster.

- Informality: Like it or not, standing on ceremony is out, casual is in— at work as well as play. A formal style of interacting that emphasizes distance is very likely to alienate many board members, especially younger ones, who have come of age in a world that prizes informality and accessibility. What in an earlier time might have been seen as dignified behavior is frequently viewed as hopelessly pompous these days. A board-savvy superintendent will, within the bounds of good taste, of course, go out of his or her way to decrease distance and promote familiarity in dealing with the board. Very often, all that is required is some thought and minor adjustments in style. For example, I worked with a superintendent who was savvy enough to rearrange her office so that meetings with individual board members were held sitting around a coffee table, rather than facing each other across her desk.

- Distrust of authority: In U.S. society, and increasingly worldwide, we no longer take for granted that institutions will act honestly or in our best interests. We assume that the executives running them are quite capable of behaving dishonestly to preserve institutional power, and we expect our trust and respect to be earned, rather than being automatically granted. There is no reason to believe that school board members come to the boardroom any more respectful or trusting than the average citizen, and board-savvy superintendents, therefore, place a premium on openness, candor, and transparency in their dealings with board members, never falling victim to the "Trust me, I'm the expert" syndrome. This might mean, for example, that you invite your board members to delve more deeply into the assumptions undergirding projected cost increases in next year's budget than you otherwise might, or that you go out of your way to explicate the possible negative ramifications of a course of action that you are recommending to the board.

In closing, I trust that you have found this brief tour of the board–superintendent partnership terrain informative and that you will be able to put the approaches and techniques that are described in the foregoing pages to practical use in your school district. The stakes are high: not only a stronger, more enduring board–superintendent partnership, but ultimately the kind of high-impact governing that these changing, challenging times in public education demand. Of course, in a small guidebook such as this, I could only hit the high points of partnership building and maintenance. However, if you really do put the board–superintendent partnership high on your priority list, I promise that this book will serve as a powerful resource, providing you with a roadmap that you can follow in building your knowledge and sharpening your skills in the partnership "business," as well as a framework within which you can analyze and draw lessons from your experience.

Best wishes for every success on your never-ending partnership odyssey!

About the Author

Doug Eadie is the founder and president of Doug Eadie & Company. During the past 25 years, Doug has consulted with more than 450 nonprofit and public organizations, including many school districts, in the areas of board and chief executive leadership and innovation/change management. Doug is the author of 14 books on public/nonprofit leadership in addition to *Eight Keys to an Extraordinary Board–Superintendent Partnership*, including *The Board-Savvy Superintendent* (with Paul Houston) and *Extraordinary Board Leadership: The Seven Keys to High-Impact Governance*. The Council for the Advancement and Support of Education (CASE) selected Doug's *Extraordinary Board Leadership* to receive its H. S. Warwick Research Award for 2002.

Before founding his consulting practice, Doug held a variety of public/nonprofit executive positions, including budget director of a large city and community college executive. He served as a Peace Corps Volunteer for three years, teaching ancient history and English at the Tafari Makonnen Secondary School in Addis Ababa, Ethiopia. Doug is a Phi Beta Kappa graduate of the University of Illinois at Urbana and received his master of science in management degree from the Weatherhead School of Management at Case Western Reserve University.

LaVergne, TN USA
14 April 2010
179263LV00001B/94/P